dead weight

dead weight

A MEMOIR IN ESSAYS

randall horton

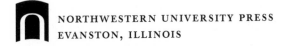
NORTHWESTERN UNIVERSITY PRESS
EVANSTON, ILLINOIS

Northwestern University Press
www.nupress.northwestern.edu

Printed in the United States of America

10 9 8 7 6 5 4 3 2 1

Library of Congress Cataloging-in-Publication Data

Names: Horton, Randall, author.
Title: Dead weight : a memoir in essays / Randall Horton.
Description: Evanston, Illinois : Northwestern University Press, 2022.
Identifiers: LCCN 2021041516 | ISBN 9780810144637 (paperback) | ISBN
    9780810144644 (ebook)
Subjects: LCSH: Horton, Randall. | African American poets—20th century—
    Biography. | African American poets—21st century—Biography. | Poets, American—
    20th century—Biography. | Poets, American—21st century—Biography. | College
    teachers—United States—Biography. | Drug dealers—United States—Biography.
Classification: LCC PS3608.O7727 Z46 2022 | DDC 811/.6—dc23
LC record available at https://lccn.loc.gov/2021041516

For Rosie Lee Davis and Elvie Horton (Big Seventy)

contents

preface and acknowledgments

This book is a work of nonfiction. The events and experiences detailed are true and have been faithfully rendered as I remember them to the best of my ability, except that some names have been changed to protect privacy. Special thanks to the following publications, in which portions of this memoir were originally published: "And So, It's Complicated," in "Persecution," ed. Reginald Dwayne Betts, special issue, *Michigan Quarterly Review* 59, no. 4 (Fall 2020); "Killing the [I] in Prison, If Only for a Moment," in Poetry Foundation blog, October 1, 2018, https://www.poetryfoundation.org/harriet-books/2018/10/killing-the-i-in-prison-if-only-for-a-moment/; and "Can Poetry Save a Life?," in Poetry Foundation blog, October 8, 2018, https://www.poetryfoundation.org/harriet-books/2018/10/can-poetry-save-a-life/.

I would like to thank the following organizations for helping to shape the narrative of *Dead Weight*: the Soze Foundation, the Civil Rights Corps, Chicago State University, the Alabama Writers' Forum, and the Poetry Center at the University of Arizona.

I would also like to thank the following people for their invaluable input and their faith in me: Lisa Allen, Kofi Antwi, Reginald Dwayne Betts, Roberto Carlos Garcia, Rubie Mariela Horton, Ashley Johnson, A. Van Jordan, Varsha Kalyani, Dr. Katie Owens-Murphy, Willie Perdomo, Theresa Recchia, Patrick Rosal, Najaya Royal, Diane Russo, Andy Smart, and Frank X Walker. Shout out to the Stairwell for keeping the bar too damn high!

This book would not have been possible without Lauren Scovel of the Laura Gross Literary Agency and Parneshia Jones of Northwestern University Press for understanding my vision for *Dead Weight*. Also, thanks to my editor, Leslie Keros, for saving me from myself.

dead weight

PART 1

The Protagonist in Somebody Else's Melodrama

The ephemeral foliage to my left, blocking the picturesque view from Riverside, is outlined by hemp dogbane, hay-scented ferns, and golden Alexanders. Before the riverbank's edge, Virginia bluebells faintly obscure the yellow water taxi sputtering southbound toward that section of lower Manhattan resembling an upside-down middle finger birding the Hudson on a New York City map. One hundred yards out over the river, seagulls pipe unpredictable trajectories in broken syntax, often suspending themselves midsentence—wading in the deaf caesura— then freefalling backward into patterns of descriptive sign language. Two BMX riders with black bikes parallel and identical in pedal rotation rapidly approach before scuttling southbound on the walkway in a muted blur, unaware of their subtext of uniformity.

At 139th, vintage flood lamps, though not lit, are pronounced, erect, and lined single file along the walkway. A mother haphazardly waves a wand of streaming bubbles while her trailing son and daughter play a game of catch-and-burst-the-bubble, long before the game of life bursts their innocuous state and reality smashes into them head on with the force of a Mack truck. There is serene music in the background, a loud congregation of finches invisible within the trees, their culminating voices singing in perfect choral structures. Diesel-engine buses join the melodious overtone with the stop and go of their compression brakes up and down Riverside Drive.

Because it is mandated by the New York City parks department to CLEAN UP AFTER YOUR DOG, there are sporadic flashes of pooper scoopers bending down with plastic bags to retrieve animal waste deposited on the walkway. A few more steps up the steep incline is 145th Street and the official entrance to Riverbank State Park, its tall, perforated metal sign bearing the park's name in bright red letters, accented by the wrought-iron gate painted green, complete with guard shack nearby—then the view to the left bends back to the brackish blue water of the Hudson before opening onto a canopy of trees, as if the impending stretch of walkway is the calm before the storm.

Dusk seems more than eager to descend on this East Coast island, and headlights will soon stab the darkness while inching across the bridge into New Jersey. The smell of yesterday's rain is crisp to inhale with each elongated stride along the walkway. At 150th Street, a small, oval-shaped park has at its center a fifteen-foot-high, ten-foot-wide, six-inch-thick bronze sculpture by Elizabeth Catlett resting on a raised bed of grass. Carved out of the slab is the silhouette of a man who has no rib cage or flesh or veins. His insides are cut out. The silhouette holds his right hand up, as if to say *stop*, while the left is anchored to his side, as if providing balance against the turbulence this world is capable of inflicting, a sort of rudder. Next to the monument is a concrete marker inscribed with these words:

> I am an invisible man . . . .
> I am invisible, understand, simply because
> people refuse to see me.

Behold Ralph Ellison's invisible man.

The silhouette, whom I will call Cutout Man, could represent me in various stages of a complicated life, at times unable to escape the social pitfalls that have befallen a slew of Black men, particularly in the '80s, an era that seems so damn archaic now. The residual damage caused by drugs and long prison sentences, however, is ever-present. I take a seat on one of the curved benches nearby and study my doppelgänger in amazement as spectator and spectacle, fanatical-like—thinking how easily the sculptor of this timeless character in somebody else's melodrama sequestered an unimaginable protagonist rendered real.

The unauthorized biographers of our (yes—mine and his) life's trajectory charted a path wrought with racism, deception, trickery, willful ambiguity, satire, and comedic relief alongside the theater of the absurd. We were only made aware of our lot in society through an accidental point of view—that moment we were able to reverse the lens and peer into twisted eyes connected to a brain that dreamed a horrific fantasy for which there seems no immediate escape. Cutout Man and I fell victim to a narrative that featured us as the tragedy, the sad sack, the bumbling idiot unable to control the thematic threads within our story line. We could not hear the hidden or silent dialogue that kept our daily existence simmering below the surface of the living.

The only difference between us is that I was born not of the pen but of the flesh; blood courses through my veins, and I am filled with bone and sinew, yet my insides, too, are as invisible as a cutout.

I get up from the bench and position myself so that I am looking into Cutout Man's eyes, before he can split the scene. On this day we are alone in New York City—Hamilton Heights, to be exact—a rarity in a city of millions. I have long held a burning desire to dialogue with this symbol of erasure about the madness that made both of us real; this is my opportunity. Although I am talking to myself, I am talking to Cutout Man. Today he will be my therapist. I can see straight through his body, clear across the Hudson River to the Jersey shoreline. He is a pattern or figure traced then cut from a human being—an outline within an outline.

Without provocation and unannounced I ask him to imagine the conclusion of a newborn's conceptualized journey through its mother's womb—how the external world, with those once unintelligible voices and inaudible mumblings, is finally brought to fruition. In this particular incidence, however, there are no cigars or floating helium balloons with IT'S A BOY! because the four-pound eleven-ounce body in question is still in question—struggling not to be dead on arrival because it arrived prematurely. Nature attempts to fulfill its obligatory promise of a robust life while the idea of "nurture" is being put to task, as in—there is nothing to facilitate this baby's nurturing except an incubator on the top floor of South Highlands Infirmary in Birmingham, Alabama. Quite an arduous voyage for the newbie to humankind, all seven months of him, shepherded from the hospital basement (a makeshift prenatal unit) where, in 1961, colored babies were delivered and thereby separated from the white race.

The infant became the only dark spot in a row of wrinkly premature newborns, standing out as society's *marked construct*—as the *other* among, well, everyone else.

An odd occurrence if a photo of this event had been presented in 2021. Layered within the Polaroid negative of the photo would exist a textbook case of critical race theory, presenting a narrative of Blackness dreamed up by the likes of the philosopher Hegel with a target of ridicule on its back—underscoring what it means to be the *other* on plastic film. We see the image of an unhealed racial wound refusing to recede into the annals of historical record.

The wound is deepened by all the white babies permitted to have their mother pick them up, hold and hug them by the butt, stare into their inquisitive eyes, do the *goochey-goo* or whatever it is that makes babies giggle and slobber on their mother's cheek. The exception is the little spot on the top floor. His mother is prohibited from walking up from the basement to participate in this bonding ritual because of the Jim Crow segregation ordinances preventing color-constructed people from mixing with whiteness in public or private.

So the mother cannot dote on her little spot. She cannot whisper, *Mommy loves you.* The two did briefly meet upon completion of the birthing procedure, but the placenta arrived first, and Little Spot was almost hung by an umbilical cord before the journey began. Never mind that in Alabama's horrid memory there are a litany of bodies strung up from structures who, before their necks snapped, wished they had died at birth.

After the placenta came the baby, his mother oblivious of his condition as the delivering doctor attempted to breathe life into the infant.

For fifteen minutes a white man who believed in and endorsed segregation placed his mouth over the baby's mouth—as if color was the last thing in the world that mattered—and gave the baby life in his body so that he might live. Fifteen minutes is an eternity of temporal space in an ever-evolving world—it is a gaping black hole. I tell Cutout Man: in that time you can write a short speech to your enemies declaring independence from the haters, damn near change a flat tire on the Sprain Brook Parkway in the Bronx, ride the No. 4 Cottage Grove (also known as Garbage Grove) bus in Chicago from Hyde Park to Bronzeville on Gwendolyn Brooks Day. You can water a bed of multihued roses, cook bacon and eggs with wheat toast, cuss out and make up with your best friend from high school in three different languages, and evidently you can breathe life into a Black baby's mouth until it catches the spirit of civilization.

When the baby caught the spirit, he was taken like so many Black bodies before him—stolen from his mother through an ordinance preventing them from bonding for eleven days.

The act hypocritical, contradictory, and *plain ignant*, as my main man Graveyard Pimp from across the railroad tracks in Titusville (pronounced *titties-ville* by the indigenous) would say before turning up a fifth of Red Dagger from the state liquor store on 6th Avenue. You must believe if Graveyard had heard this history about a white man in the Southside neighborhood of Birmingham breathing into a premature Black baby for fifteen minutes to jumpstart life, then segregating him by the laws of ignorance from his mother for eleven days, Grave would've reflected, then offered without further comment, "Mane, how you gone sit there and tell me some bullshit like that?" before slugging the 21 percent wine down his throat again.

Do you know how the baby came to exist as the only dark spot in an infirmary ward full of whiteness? The explanation goes as such: on October 15, 1961, at the Catholic church bingo game in the Smithfield section of Birmingham, a cousin, Sherry, all of one year old, wriggling and being held by the soon-to-be-mother—trying to break free from authority, like all babies do—inadvertently kicked the seven-months-pregnant mother in the stomach, who thought nothing of the jolt at the time. Later, at the soon-to-be-grandmother Rosie Lee Davis's bootleg house on 8th Avenue North, the lady who lived directly in the back facing the alley, Ellen Stewart—who went by Two-Bit or the Smithfield Stewart Press (didn't a decibel of gossip escape her ears)—decided she needed to walk twenty yards from her shotgun house to Rosie Lee's clapboard to deliver important breaking news.

Two-Bit first had to pass the tall, thick-rooted pecan tree whose archaic branches and thin leaves cascaded over the black dirt driveway. She could not sidestep the old-timers born before or at the turn of the twentieth century who sat under the tree's soaking shade, sipping beers wrapped in white napkins. Two-Bit then entered through the back screen door, where she ran smack into the essence of Black life: folks who worked hard to drink hard to live hard. She walked past the kitchen where they were selling pig-ear sandwiches drenched in Tabasco sauce and drinking fifty-cent shots of red whiskey, past the middle room where couples paid three bucks for fifteen minutes of animalistic sex, right to Rosie Lee's big room in the front, where she declared, "You betta watch that gal, it's a full moon out tonight."

Evidently the moon did a bowlegged jig, howled—and at midnight the pregnant mother found herself rushed to South Highlands, two months ahead of schedule. Although South Highlands Infirmary had separate sections for white and nonwhite patients, and for children with disabilities, there would be no time to set up an incubator in the Black ward, and so the infant's journey upstairs, minus the mother, began. Because no mother came to brush the baby's hair, the nurses molded the baby in their perceived immaculate image, little pompadour and all.

Bodies, or more specifically Black bodies, are tied to the condition that creates or renders erased bodies visible along time's continuum. None of the nurses had ever cared for a premature Black baby, so the only compass became memory through an alternative lens with colonial rhetoric dictating their belief and ideology. In other words, the nurses nurtured a baby they didn't believe existed, unwittingly reinforcing the idea of color, and with each delicate stroke of the brush, the baby built resentment festering between anger and evil, a resentment soon to be manifested in the larger world. With every indoctrination into whiteness, the nurses gave license to the baby's soon-to-be Blackness.

An eleven-day separation of mother and baby is indeed criminal, but, as you know, Cutout Man, the collective memory of African Americans reveals a much harsher tale: the Black body as disposable commodity or good. At four pounds and eleven ounces, the disposable body needed to weigh five pounds before the mother could pick the baby up and let Little Spot know he had not been erased from memory. For eleven days straight, a painstaking telephone call came from 127 8th Avenue North in Smithfield—a stone's throw from Dynamite Hill, where houses exploded into splinters upon detonation because they were occupied by Black people—inquiring about the baby's weight. Each day the twenty-four-year-old clutched the rotary phone, placed her index finger in the corresponding numerical holes, dialed the seven digits clockwise, and waited for a nurse on duty to pick up.

The mother then strained above vulgar-talking men and women, drunk on liquor, to hear the magical word: *come.*

Each *not yet* brought uncontrollable tears; yet the fact that Little Spot lived was reason for hope. The mother had moved back home to have the baby—having long ago left a lineage of bootlegging women to attend college and obtain a bachelor's degree in education from Alabama A&M. All of that and back home until the husband could find a job closer to Birmingham. The husband and wife had a baby, but they didn't, but she called and called until five pounds ended the legal separation and the hospital said, *Come.* During those eleven days *West Side Story* would premiere at New York City's Rivoli Theatre. Thurgood Marshall would be sworn in as a judge on the US Court of Appeals for the Second Circuit. Chubby Checker would perform "The Twist" on *The Ed Sullivan Show.*

The mother could not have cared less about these soon-to-be events—the only "twist" she was interested in came on the eleventh day.

When my mother and father brought me to 127 8th Avenue North as a newborn, having survived an eleven-day stretch of touch-and-go, the tininess of my infant body frightened people, especially children. Catbird, a rail-thin man who never appeared in public without a fedora tilted back on his head—who remained a frequent fixture in Rosie Lee's bootleg house throughout my formative years—took one look at the little spot and said, "Eunice Pearl, that baby ain't big as a muskeeta." From that day forward, my nickname would be Skeeter. I didn't know it then, during the sepia age of the '60s, but I was being conditioned early to confront and overcome situations based on skin color, and to accept that, contrary to popular belief, color would define my lifelong existence. I could not enter that world and say I didn't see color when my birth had been defined by it.

This conditioning prepared me for the days, weeks, months of isolation where I would be tucked away in a prison cell, segregated and deemed unfit for society.

The poet Lucille Clifton would one day write the poem "Won't You Celebrate with Me" with her own struggles in mind, and I would come to identify with the last four lines, which prophetically sing,

> come celebrate
> with me that everyday
> something has tried to kill me
> and has failed.

Being placed in a controlled environment for days perhaps hinted at a future to be realized in adult prison thirty-seven years later, a parallel between child and adult that would dictate who I would become.

The second forced detainment would be spent in lockdown twenty-three hours a day at Baltimore Receiving Unit, a facility where prisoners were assigned and classified. Days blended into one long stretch of lockouts and lock-ins. I discovered language in books like *Fathering Words,*

Convicted in the Womb, *The Autobiography of Malcolm X*, and *Makes Me Wanna Holla*. These books demanded I create my own language to break out of the prison I encapsulated myself in, so I wrote words on yellow legal pads to escape.

Perhaps a standing ovation? Maybe whistles and cheers or a full-page congratulatory in the New York Times? *Is this what you come to tell me? Surely there must be more?*

The bronze silhouette doesn't articulate this aloud, but I know his heart and capacity for caring were ripped out decades ago, and I am certain he is unmoved. Come on, Cutout Man, damn! I respectfully raise my voice to gain his undivided attention before I walk back to the wooden bench, sit, and place my head in my folded hands, as if darkness is a prescription for solace. I want him to be empathetic, but I know I am standing in the pulpit with my back to the congregation, preaching old news to the choir. After all the years gone by, I am still trying to make sense of race—or the idea of race—that lives in the mind of humans.

But do you know many have made this pilgrimage not only to see themselves visible, but to witness how one is memorialized alongside the progress of history?

The man cannot talk, but we are having a conversation, a meeting of the minds in this circular park on the West Side of New York City. We are inanimate and animate. We exist, but then we do not. We are material matter known as Black matter(s). Unlike my statuesque idol's grandfather, my grandmother did not speak in metaphors and never told me to "kill 'em with kindness" on her deathbed. I admit: yes, there is more, but give me a minute to gather my thoughts. This is not easy.

In order to talk about myself I need to step outside myself. Again, point of view is important. If I rise from this park bench and gravitate toward the Hudson River, I am able to stare straight through the bronze cutout to the horizon at West 150th Street and Broadway. Any alteration of view allows for postwar tenements with identical red fire escapes on either side to bleed into the cutout space where bone and cartilage should be. Rotating our would-be lens 180 degrees, the newly formed view offers azaleas and dogwoods, presenting an alternate reality that could bring Cutout Man alive. I walk over to the sculpture.

I am calmer and speak in a measured tone about my relationship to the Black aesthetic, the "common folk" Langston Hughes hinted at in "The Negro Artist and the Racial Mountain."

I tell Cutout Man what he already knows, and that is that grand-mothers are the first to spoil a newborn baby. They are the owners of stern callous hands filled with wisdom, the bridge between mother and child. Because I almost hanged in happenstance at birth but lived, over time I grew into my grandmother's miracle grandchild. I would be afforded the elasticity to venture within the man-made world of patri-archy and racism, to understand and conquer that which would—and had—tried to kill me. There would be numerous failures, but my grand-mother understood the Black male's faults and plight better than he did, that in order to participate in this social experiment called America, social realities needed to be negotiated and realized. In order to get over to get even, she knew I would need to understand who put the barriers in place, who made color a dichotomy, and why. The proverbial apple didn't fall or roll too far from the tree that bore it.

On the paternal side, there was my dad's father, Elvie Horton, or Big Seventy, who cooked moonshine in a vat and ran liquor from Attalla to Guntersville, Alabama.

The Great Depression knocked on everyone's door by 1931 and with-out recourse—this difficult time in American history banged hard on Big Seventy's, a man who had no choice but to turn water into liquid gold. My grandfather saw no moral dilemma in selling moonshine to live like a human being. His reasoning proved to be no different from mine in the mid- to late '80s, after hope turned to anger with the discovery that the only way to capture the carrot-dangling American dream was through a beige rock designed to destroy the Blackness that raised me. But rent, gas, cable, and electric needed to be paid on a monthly basis despite lim-ited economic opportunities. Same for a young Big Seventy in 1931—the only difference being alcohol instead of cocaine. Foreshadowing the men of the '80s, Big Seventy ended up incarcerated, working on the chain gang in 1932—an early participant in what would eventually be called the prison-industrial complex.

One could say that the boy inherited the collective fate of the Black male experience—incarceration—pointing to the paternal grandfather's arrest and conviction.

That would be a good enough excuse for my stay in state prison, except that this rationalization would preempt the narrative of the Black woman who operated outside the social and gender roles assigned to her. Perhaps for someone who went to jail for illegal activity, operating below the surface to stay surface level, Big Seventy seems to be the perfect example. But Big Seventy could have sat in the Baptist choir on a Sunday morning and sang, "Precious Lawd, take my hand / Lead me on, let me stand . . ." in comparison to my grandmother, Rosie Lee, who bought state store whiskey then resold it to her loyal patrons, ran numbers, and rented rooms on-site for people to fuck. She sold fish, pig-ear, and pig-tail sandwiches on Fridays—and paid the police off with weekly contributions to the Birmingham Municipal Fund, as evidenced by the meticulous receipt book she kept.

Rosie Lee believed in customer service. She understood you gotta give to get.

My grandmother gave credit on the dollar, got mean when need be, and wasn't shy about using the double-barreled .22 in the chifforobe. Then there were the rooms. Rooms men and women entered, some trying not to be seen, sneaking through the front and back doors; others not giving a damn, preferring to let everyone know they were getting laid by somebody else's main squeeze. I began pouring fifty-cent and dollar shots of "red" and "white" from the kitchen pantry by the age of eight—by ten I was changing bedsheets and emptying piss pots after Rosie Lee knocked on the door and yelled, "Time!"

The daily tasks I performed in my grandmother's house as a child did not affect the importance of attending school, not stealing, having proper manners, and so on. Her foundation of wrong-while-right helped create a mindset I would adopt at the height of the cocaine infiltration in America in the '80s, which would incorporate how to organize and sustain (in the midst of so many closed doors) a skill that relied on blending into the urban underworld—making shady men and women believe they were getting something for nothing. This would be my grandmother's gift to a Black boy who would enter the cutthroat existence of the '80s.

I grew up in my grandmother's house mainly because my parents were schoolteachers and she, being without a nine-to-five, was the only person my mother trusted to watch her child. Over the years, from the time I was able to reason and observe, I noticed the assortment of characters who paraded through the house every day, some comical and some tragic, like Bookie, who moved into my grandmother's house to take her former boyfriend Bluejay's place after his stroke left him sideways, dead as a doorknob, on her bed. It took two days to figure out that no one in the family liked Bookie—we thought he was successfully living off my grandmother's dime. Bookie rose every morning at five o'clock, filled the entire house with the rancid odor of Blue Magic shaving cream, and scraped his bald head with a butter knife. Then he put on Liberty denim overalls like he was going to work, except that was the problem—he didn't have a job.

By noon his lip drug the floor like the tongue of a construction boot— worn, faded, and mummified from all the gin soaked up. By six Bookie was ignant and a natural fool.

Then there was Catbird, the person that gave me the name Skeeter, who religiously wore dark seersucker suits, white shirts, and felt hats. This small, lanky man possessed the uncanny ability to make the most serious situation humorous, like the times he got paid on a Friday and by Saturday morning his pants pockets drooped like rabbit ears while he swung in the doorway of my grandmother's bedroom, asking if he could get a fifty-cent shot of red on credit, his body resembling a damaged toothpick. Bent in a half-moon, he would rock back and forth, crooning, "Teach me how to swim, Rosie Lee; I can drown with the best of 'em."

Dot was totally different from Bookie and Catbird in that, first, she was a woman, and second, she actually tried to be an ally to my grand-mother instead of drinking up all the liquor.

A portly woman who wore knit pants so tight they looked like brush-strokes on her uneven body, Dot instilled the fear of God in some men and most women. On days when Bookie was too drunk and Grandma too tired and I was not around, Dot took the pantry keys to where the liquor stayed locked on three wooden shelves and dispensed it as requested. Dot put the paper money under her large breast. Every time she dug to give somebody change, I wondered what it felt like to be a quarter under so much weight in her bra. Dot could also play the hell out of some spades.

Spades games were especially exciting after the jukebox man made his monthly rounds to bring new 45s and exhaust the music machine of its nickels, dimes, and quarters.

Men and women would allow this interloper, the color of bleached bones, into their personal space, which did not include whiteness. The jukebox man was essential to their existence but out of place like apples on a lemon tree. See, through music he determined the rhythm of their blues, the octave of voices in card games, or who became Jody on any given night. It would be years later when I learned "Jody" to be another name for a man sleeping with somebody else's woman. The jukebox man perpetually carried platters of Black gold, where artists like Aretha Franklin, James Brown, Bobby Blue Bland, B.B. King, and Little Johnny Taylor hid in the sleeveless jackets of his Pandora's box.

While the latest 45s spun, patrons enjoyed the music with head nods and dangling cigarettes, playing spades while their lips sucked on liquor in small white cups and cans or bottles of beer. One card game I remember went something like this: Isaac, a chocolate-skinned, bald-headed man with a raspy voice, slapped his leadoff card on the wafer-thin card table. It spun north by east, revealing a ten of hearts.

"You gotta brang ass to get ass," Sledge offered with a pull, flick, and release of a jack of hearts. Her occupation was digging fingers into women's scalps with Crown Royal Grease at Deluxe Beauty Shop one block down the street on 8th Avenue.

Understanding the mandate given, Bookie drew from his third-grade education, throwing out a six of spades with no eye contact. He banged his fist on the table and yelled, "That's right! I dranks Johnny Walker Red. Sledge, get your money ready, darlin', and by the way, your old, wrinkled ass safe with me." Before ripples of laughter surrounded the room, Dot's forehead became glued to the ace of spades. Her neck rotated 90 degrees for the men to view while she hissed, "How 'bout kissing my natural Black ass, muthafucka. Get on up from here, nigga! Next!"

Okay, so when do we get to the good stuff? Stop holding out! Cutout Man is no fool. He does not laugh. There is more. He knows it. We wade deep in the uncomfortable silence.

He is waiting for the acknowledgment, the narrative of the moment when I realized there was no way to live an enchanted life, one where race did not need to be talked about, a life where color would not dictate how I moved through the world. Yes. Yes. Yes. I was indeed naive about race until I experienced the moment of which you are thinking and know to be true. I am a student of literature, however, and not completely blind to moments that make race real. In Richard Wright's *Native Son* one only has to place himself in the shoes of Bigger Thomas or, even better still, in the hands that lay Mary Dalton to rest in her bed after a night of drinking with her friends. Bigger is the chauffeur—a job he cannot lose—but also, Bigger cannot shake the undeniable reality that a Black man should not be in a white woman's bedroom in the early part of the twentieth century. I tell Cutout Man to think about the informed hands of Bigger when Mary's blind grandmother enters the room. The grandmother cannot see, but she can hear, and to be heard is to risk what Bigger knows through historical record.

Historical memory comes rushing via the blood, all that genealogy from the first cornfield holler to the late-night arwhoolies.

It is in the codespeak of DNA, and it is this polemic-driven memory that encourages hands to stuff the pillow over Mary's face, careful she doesn't scream in her drunken stupor, careful she keeps the silence even if it means death. It is the shudder in Bigger, a moment so dominant it defies the rational, bordering on the irrational and the stupid, invoking something unique and terrifying to the Black experience. For further illustration, let us turn to Toni Morrison's *Beloved*, in which Sethe, faced with the prospect of returning her children to slavery after enjoying a time of freedom, knowing that outside the barn doors drummed the undeniable hoofbeats of those who would enslave her again, does the unthinkable. I could not even imagine having the hands that held the hacksaw to kill my daughter, my beloved.

When I read this passage, I had to ask what memory could be so demonstrably strong as to terminate your own child's life? Maybe it was the brutality of rape or the constant humiliation of the body, or maybe it was the refusal to live as *other* that made Sethe kill her own child. And yet, Beloved is more than a memory. She is a metaphor for that which refuses to die. As a character in literature and given the relation-ship between Ellison and Wright, Cutout Man must know all this, but I wanted him to know I know; and yet, at one time, I did not.

Cutout Man, I do not mean to insult your intelligence. This was the emphatic statement: "Find me somewhere, 'cause I ain't going to school with white people no mo'!"

The directive, or more specifically, this direct order coming out of the mouth of my ten-year-old self, didn't pull punches about inner feelings, nor did it delve into great detail with vivid imagery, nor did it provide reasoning behind the sudden departure request, other than what they, the parents, already knew. The statement was blurted out without the lit-any of complaints because that would ring rhetorical—like a dog chasing its tail. You see, it would have been useless to list the numerous times I heard "Hey, nigger!" in the fifth grade while walking down the hill from the middle school to the K–3 section where my mother taught so that we could go home at the end of the day, or the various occasions I dodged and zigzagged rocks thrown at my head, or the unrestricted side-eyes and mean-spirited stares from the kids who did not look like me.

Believe me. The weight of carrying race when no one else around you carries race is daunting, draining. It creates an inner anger that, once unleashed, is an unmitigated force.

Although *Brown v. Board of Education* was decided in 1954, some schools and districts waited until the early '70s to desegregate. In Birmingham, Alabama, or the Magic City, that glowing republic of Southern oligarchy, compliance came in the waning hours in the fall of '72. This desegregation included integrating teachers, which brought me, the ten-year-old, to the emphatic statement about white people.

My mother and I entered Gardendale Elementary as a social experiment of integration mandated by the Supreme Court, and I would soon come to find out what it meant to be Black. There is a wonderful video of James Baldwin debating William F. Buckley at Cambridge University on the argument that "the American dream has been achieved at the expense of the American Negro." The event was hosted by the Cambridge Union, a student debating society, in 1965, four years after my birth at the segregated South Highlands Infirmary in Southside. There is a moment, about eighteen minutes into the video, when Baldwin articulates:

> In the case of an American Negro, born in that glittering republic—and in the moment you are born, since you don't know any better, every stick and stone and every face is white, and since you have not yet seen a mirror, you suppose that you are too—it comes as a great shock, around the age of five or six or seven, to discover [that] the flag to which you have pledged allegiance, along with everybody else, has not pledged allegiance to you. It comes as a great shock to discover that [as] Gary Cooper [is] killing off the Indians, [and] you are rooting for Gary Cooper, that the Indians were you.

The thing is, Cutout Man, before my entry into Gardendale, every time I pledged allegiance in a classroom, it had been with kids who looked like me, kids I learned to high-five, dap up, and shoot marbles between shotgun houses with as we meandered into our teenage years.

Did you know that Toni Morrison took the position that something was lost in segregation? The "lost" doesn't celebrate the division racism produces but what came out of that division: a way of going against the grain for the sake of the self's survival. Taking the Blackness forced upon you—the nigga that you became—and making it valuable, something to be studied, imitated, appropriated, and commodified within contemporary culture for the sake of modern art.

Me and the kids I once pledged allegiance with were being conditioned to blindly pledge loyalty to a system we hadn't begun to understand, nor had that system pledged allegiance to us.

There had been dynamite blasts, water hoses thrust upon the throngs, billy club beatings, dog bites, hangings, insurrections against humanity, and violence right in our own city; and yet, we remained oblivious to the outer world of segregation, encapsulated in our own subsociety of a perceived otherness. Maybe if we kids had been aware, or if our parents had been more woke, we all would have revolted against this narrative, or at least questioned this insane allegiance to a society not yet fully committed to our best interest.

And yes, I would watch the old Westerns with my father, cheering for the cowboys to do the Indians dirty. Even outside playing with my friends between the shotgun houses in Smithfield, I strutted a six-shooter cap gun with full cowboy suit, thinking I could be the Lone Ranger, when actually all I could ever hope to be was Tonto, a sidekick. What Baldwin knew—and I didn't, but would soon find out—was that there is a terrifying moment in one's system of reality, a moment that will contextualize race, from which there is no return.

True, you do become the thing to be hunted and treated like an animal. The trauma is difficult to remember and retell.

I begin slow, meek: then it happened. *Say what? I can't hear you. Speak a little louder!* Cutout Man is pushing the story out of my mouth. *Don't hold back now. Get it out. Speak!!!* I come back again with: then it happened! *That's it. Now we talkin'!* I continue with authority: The ball was up in the air, and Michael Hallmark, my new best white friend, had thrown the spiral perfectly. I was so fast I thought I would jump out of my PF Flyers, and they were laced real tight. I wanted to jump high but couldn't jump high enough because the ball was sailing too far for my fingertips to reach it. The ball hit a girl on her side. I went to pick the ball up. She kicked real hard. Called me "nigger." Called me "nigger." She called me a nigger—and I punched her in the mouth with my fist. Hard. Red appeared on her face. Red blood rolling down her white face. She started crying. I started laughing. I wanted to cry. She called me "nigger" and I hit her real hard and it felt damn good.

Let me be clear. Eunice Pearl Davis, now a Horton but daughter of Rosie Lee, was never a timeout or stand-in-the-corner type of mother.

My mother never hesitated to give teachers full authorization to paddle without parental consent when deemed necessary. I have no memory of how I arrived at the principal's office to wait for punishment—maybe it was the eerie silence surrounding the "event" because the teachers knew something I did not in terms of the history related to Black boys and white women in the South. The memory of what transpired after my arrival is clear: Eunice Pearl comes into the office and says to the principal standing over me, "Do not lay one hand on him." When I say *never*, I mean never ever did Eunice Pearl utter those words in regard to punishment. I knew then, in this racialized moment, my response to an action was bigger than the act. But Baldwin knew there would come a time, and that time had arrived.

It would take a few orbits around the sun for me to understand the enormous weight, the intensity of the primal scene that could've taken my life.

Forget two years after the eleven-day segregation from my mother, but then don't—how on September 15, 1963, a Sunday morning dynamite blast inside a church morphed four little girls into a forever memory. Forget Carol Denise McNair, but don't. Forget Addie Mae Collins, but don't. Forget Cynthia Wesley, but don't. Forget Carole Robertson, but don't, and don't forget Black boys.

There is always a lineage of Black boys to draw context from too. There had been Virgil Ware, sitting on the handlebars of his brother's bicycle, who caught a bullet in the chest from a shooter riding shotgun on the back of a Confederate flag–bearing motorbike. The end result: face down in a ditch. James Robinson, angered by the church bombing because he had already experienced the moment of race realization, gunned down two hours after the blast in an alley—and make no mistake, the police account matters more than the victim.

The usual responses came after the fact: he lunged, reached, looked suspicious, made a move—they always flee—the police fired in the air, fired in self-defense, because niggas be magical, niggas hang themselves by themselves, turn water into wine, slip out of handcuffs, be looking like every other nigga, do other niggas' time in jail: real and imagined, make freedom disappear in a finger snap, or turn it into a life sentence; or, worse yet, niggas get shot dead and the world changes the television channel, unbothered, unfettered, unmoved.

My father, who left work with the ghost of Emmett Till on his mind when he got the call from Gardendale Elementary that I hit a white girl, would years later admit: *He had to go.*

Had to. He *had to* because I was in a place that didn't want me, that said "Hey, nigger" every day to discourage me from falling in love with their idea of beauty, their idea of truth, to never mistake Blackness for whiteness in terms of privilege. The principal wanted integration, was part of a movement in Birmingham for equal education and access, perhaps was a dreamer in believing that all men and women were created equal. In his dream he saw the need to protect this Black boy from a fate all too clear for Black boys who didn't stay in line. The principal called a meeting with my father and the girl's parents. The parents wanted blood or neck and were not at all happy their little girl (with blood coagulated on her face and lips) got clocked in the mouth by a nigger, but neither was the Black boy happy at being called "nigger," so we sat in the conundrum.

In the end, the principal sided with his gut, the question being, what had I done wrong? My parents taught me not to hate. I did not call the girl trailer trash or any of the derogatory terms I would come to know as an adult. Perhaps the principal had no choice if this social experiment was going to have the opportunity to work. But what about the below-the-surface narrative (by those who often control the narrative) whispering in the parents' ears: *You know, he can go missing, done happened before. Turn up in the Coosa River with his face eaten by catfish.*

I will never know how close I came to being seen at sunup with my neck snapped in Kelly Ingram Park, hanging from a makeshift wooden cross.

I would go back to school the next day like nothing happened, that big-ass elephant no one wanted to acknowledge in the room, still present and accounted for. The kids knew what happened. I knew what happened, yet not one of the adults wanted to talk about it openly. No one cared to ask me about the trauma of that moment, the fact that I hit a girl when all my life I had been told that was the one thing never to do.

After that incident, I didn't associate with the other kids in my class. I only wanted to get as far from that racial madness as humanly possible, because it became evident these people were incapable of being human. I never saw the girl again. Maybe her parents took her out of school, unhappy at how white folks cared about the fate of Black boys in Jefferson County. One thing I am almost certain of, and would love to confirm years later: the little white girl never called anyone a nigger again.

The next year, sixth grade—I would stroll into an all-Black Catholic school planted directly in the hood, across the tracks in Titusville. Thank God.

There would be bonding over stacked heels and platforms, circular Afros and braided cornrows. We would drown each other in code-switching language, the way we said *mane* and *gull*, and we didn't run from our own skin; as a matter of fact, we ran into it headfirst. We were in a cocoon of Blackness, and whiteness had inverted to the *other*—they were the others now, and we called each other nigga, but it was love, learning early in life to take what is given and turn it into something valued. I'd left hell and returned to a mythological paradise, if only for a moment. And yet, society would not care about the scars, the racial wounds bandaged up—but would expect me to forgive those who knew damn well what they were doing.

Cutout Man, as you know, Birmingham isn't a popular American city for major novels or film productions. Usually, when a person hears *Birmingham*, they instantly think segregation, Bull Connor, water hoses, German shepherds biting little kids, the scourge of racism manifested in white solidarity. That Black folk in this Southern city have always been subjugated and relegated to an *otherness* from which there is no reconciliation.

Whenever I fly in to the Birmingham-Shuttlesworth International Airport from LaGuardia, I make it a point to rent a car and take the long way to my parents' house, first veering toward I-65 South from I-20 West, then getting off at 6th Avenue, crossing the railroad tracks into Smithfield. I like to take in the old viridian shotgun houses still standing in neat rows.

These were scanty wooden structures that offered a straight shot from the front door to the back: open the door into the living room and the next room would be the bedroom, then the kitchen, then the bathroom, then out the back door into a yard with a clothesline pole. Most Black folk who worked in the steel plants rented these lodgings from slum landlords such as Otey Real Estate. Segregation made Smithfield an all-Black community with a few Jewish grocery stores that catered to Black folk. My grandmother's house at 127 8th Avenue North has long been torn down, and there is nothing left but the foundation of a building that was once one of the most famous juke joints in town.

The one thing Birmingham taught me, and perhaps herein lies my fascination for a city so complicated, is that I never questioned what it meant to be a Black American in the South.

Birmingham conditioned me in a way that has never left me feeling insecure about my pigmentation, why it does and doesn't matter. I've never been confused about this aspect of my reality. When I left Birmingham, I began to see other shades of Blackness and came to understand that there were many who grew up having to ask the question, Am I Black enough?

I grew up in a sepia landscape, where black and white were the colors that dominated my pupils from first sight until well into my double-digit years. No one in my immediate family ever taught me to look at the world through a white gaze as if it would be the secret formula to a prosperous and meaningful life.

Blackness was always the center through which I moved. My kindergarten was all Black, the first elementary school I attended was all Black, and so was the high school I graduated from in 1979. I went to all-Black summer camps, played on all-Black sports teams, never once questioning the idea of Black or Blackness. People who did not grow up in Birmingham often make disparaging assumptions about how Black people grew up, let alone survived, which I find interesting, given every city I've lived in has been filled with racism, whether out in the open or disguised by an invisible dialogue that exposed itself most notably through economics and housing.

Perhaps I am a product of history, unable to escape the social structures that allowed my Blackness to be real and not imagined. I can tell that Cutout Man is thinking, *Yes, you are.*

Racism taught me to hold on to my Blackness, and now, at a time when color is being rethought as an idea dreamed up in the minds of white men, it is an idea that is nonnegotiable in my life. Smithfield is more of a ghost town at this point in history, the result of many Black people in the neighborhood going to college, having better job opportunities, and being able to participate in the housing market. All-white neighborhoods have been supplanted with Blackness, causing white flight to fly farther and farther away from the city limits.

Whenever I tell people I was born and raised in Birmingham, I get a condescending look, as if to say, *I'm sorry*. I used to fall for this sentimentality, but nowadays, it is I who feel sorry for the sympathizers because they have been lulled into a trap. I live here in New York City, one of the most literary and culturally diverse places in the country; and yet, I can walk out of my tenement on 136th and bear witness to racism and discrimination all day long. Just because you don't hear the word *nigger* doesn't mean a nigger doesn't exist within the eyes of people walking up and down your block.

I will admit that being culturally deprived harmed me, and it took years before I understood other people's idea of Blackness, or what it meant to come from the African Diaspora. At one time I thought Birmingham Black was the only kind of Black; now I know better than to make this narrow assumption, yet I am shaped to this day by a sense of belonging to a particular region, in a particular time, to a particular set of circumstances. It is often said the idea of Blackness is an avant-garde phenomenon, a never-ending reconfiguration, a color adjusting to the contours of society while leaning toward another destination—an arrival and departure—always shape-shifting for the sake of self, for the sake of survival.

I am in the epilogue years and the path forward is not dictated by anyone but me. In the end, perhaps there is no escaping the history one was destined to create. We are historical beings.

My epiphanous journey began with an incubator simulating a cell, then a prison sentence that placed me in an actual cell, forcing me to seek some semblance of freedom. Even after the release from that confined structure of iron and brick, I came to discover, or more importantly recognize, the ways in which society has kept me tethered to the state, both physical and governmental, the elasticity of the rope given to my freedom—a constant reminder that there are boundaries, an electric fence. *There may be hope for you yet.* I can now feel the vibration of approval in my bones—finally.

Race matters, and there is no outrunning a lived reality. Cutout Man knows this predicament, understands the context of my pilgrimage, because every Black man is a protagonist in somebody else's melodrama.

There is always a scene, a setting, a backstory. Today my life is compounded by the effects of racism and incarceration, yet I managed not to be a statistic, not to be stuck in an ever-present stasis, unable to free myself from the invisible clutches of a system that would chew and spit me out raw. The reason I am here, Cutout Man, is that I need you to hear me—I mean really listen and stand not in idle judgment but as an ally, one who has endured the fire and can relate to the charred edges without uttering a word.

I think back to the incubator and the disposable boy as commodified good who never stood a chance in a segregated hospital—kept alive within the balance of national guilt.

I discovered in solitary confinement that the hole is not dark matter or a circle but a possible gateway. I needed to step into 1961 as part of my reconciliation with that past. I needed to flash back to witness in order to testify. My life represents a predictable future for boys who grow up seeing color because race indoctrination begins at birth, as the Black body is innately conditioned against the Stars and Stripes: the red, white, and blue. The concrete slab cold, the metal cold. The baby cries and color doesn't fade in a cell.

If anything, Cutout Man has helped me wrestle with why we always begin with or make a case for bodies—or, more specifically, why the Black body is linked to an inherent condition that fosters invisibility. The boy grows up in a poststructural box, a perfect how-to-kill-someone blueprint. And I know now that for the sake of the morally high minded—the good—a cell is a cell to protect the righteous order. The precise moment of my birth was a foreshadowing of the time I would spend in Baltimore City Detention Center, locked in solitary for twenty-three hours a day.

I have to leave. I'm thinking that what I have poured out of my heart is symbolic of the blues. With my back turned I hear, *Who knows but that, on the lower frequencies, I speak for you?*

The last line in *Invisible Man,* and perhaps this lifelong narrative, this unorthodox way of moving through the world: the detours, roadblocks, pitfalls—and to overcome it all—is not my story alone, but one that needs to be told over and over again until we get it right, until we are all seen as human through one lens that incorporates the collective *we* of the living. These are the last words Cutout Man wants me to know, the *I speak for you* echoing back up the walkway from which I came, and I am thinking: the complaint, the effect, the resolution.

Maybe my diatribe is a lament. Maybe color will eat my Black ass alive. Maybe there are experiences I will live and die with and never understand. Maybe I will forever linger between arriving and departing, stuck in media res—always a-holding.

Holding to hold on. There is no soundtrack in my departure, only the song of leaves shimmering against the soon-to-be-gone breeze. I turn around to get one last look. Maybe Cutout Man is waving good-bye, trying to tell me to be one with nature, that we are all connected and that a character in a novel speaks for me. I don't know if I will ever come to a full understanding of race; however, I do think about a question once posed to me by a very good friend, who asked, What benefits of race am I not willing to give up?

PART 2

November 2 and a Mother's Love

On November 2, 2008, I cast a ballot for the first time in my life.

I was forty-seven years old, an age by which I should have already voted in seven presidential elections. One reason for my noncompliance with this dutiful act originated from my intimate association with what Langston Hughes referred to in "The Negro Artist and the Racial Mountain" as "the low-down folks, the so-called common element"—that subjugated class living on the fringes between the erased and the invisible, a subdivision of Blackness that has always resented the dominant narrative of whiteness. Those in the common element, a hidden society within Blackness, didn't and still don't trust legalities or due process; they will engage in illegal activity in protest against a system dedicated to making them go through hell to enjoy their civil liberties. They, or specifically we common folk, placed no blind faith in a government that had failed to make us feel like full citizens, so our motto to this very day is fuck-a-law, fuck apologies, fuck the Bill of Rights, fuck forgiveness, and fuck all those who benefited from plantations and generational wealth.

In the eyes of the common folk, whiteness was (and still is) the real illegal. The only presidential administration I remember following closely was that of Ronald Reagan, mainly because of the mandatory federal sentencing guidelines implemented to combat the rise of crack cocaine and the so-called war on drugs—a domestic drug war that arose, in part, because of the CIA's involvement with the contras in Nicaragua.

Imagine the CIA's facilitating and benefiting from the sale of cocaine smuggled into the United States, and Black men receiving ten, twenty, thirty years as a byproduct. These acts came off the heels of COINTELPRO, an FBI-led counterintelligence program that sought to destroy, among others, Black revolutionary organizations and public figures fighting for an equality that posed a threat to the American status quo.

CIA drug trafficking had to be the ultimate setup in a long list of setups perpetrated by whites against Black people. Flood the inner city with cocaine, get Black folks hooked, create the illusion of a pathway to the American dream, and then lock them up for chasing a deception. The common folk I associated with were blinded by this fool's gold and did not pay attention to the political fervor of a nation. Every action and reaction needed to be based on the relationship between dollars and cents.

Like them, I did not give a good goddamn who was president, vice president, secretary of state, senator, or city councilor.

In my self-proclaimed rebellion against the state and a version of capitalism that didn't work for me or for many of those who once worked eight hours a day for below-average wages, I adopted the philosophy of illegal. Illegal meant the opportunity to even the playing field, to buy clothes and drive a car and pay the rent or mortgage without worrying if the minimum-wage paycheck would cover the monthly bills. After years of illegal activity, I was given a prison sentence for crimes against the state. Had I been judged by a group of my peers who understood the struggles created by so many facets of racism, I would have been proclaimed innocent and free to go. But the criminal justice system doesn't work that way. I would like to say that prison rehabilitated me, but that would be a lie. I began to rehabilitate myself through writing at Montgomery County Correctional Facility, also known as Seven Locks, in 1998 as I awaited trial.

Sitting in a circle of detained citizens in the county jail, I was asked to write about my life in ways I could never express as a young, angry Black man.

In the male housing unit, social workers led a writing workshop where each participant had to get gut level to face their faults and wrongdoings. I can honestly say that writing set me on a path to freedom. One could argue that prison saved me, because on the outside, the statistical odds of escaping my environment without being shot dead did not tilt in my favor. I am very aware of this since I myself tried to kill someone who was saved only by the grace of trajectory, the bullet piercing the windshield and entering the van but missing the aorta, the kidney, the rib cage, and the throat; and yes, if it could've been them, it could've been me. A bullet was out there, lodged in a clip, waiting for a forefinger to squeeze the trigger and grant me eternal silence.

Upon sentencing in 1999, I was sent to Roxbury Correctional Institution, the state prison in Hagerstown, Maryland. When I was released in 2000, I mistakenly believed my debt had been paid to society.

I would soon come to find that the kind of debt I paid is not easily erased in the consciousness of America. Prison and the government had given me a check to cash, and as Martin Luther King Jr. noted during his "I Have a Dream" speech in Washington, DC, on the promise of America, there were insufficient funds. This attitude confirmed my complex relationship with this nation, because I believe there has always been an inadequate and unsatisfactory commitment when it comes to addressing the problems within the Black community. When I returned with the branded mark of incarceration—the F-word, *felon*—I began to see the ways in which America engages in trickery and deception, much like a shell game in which the pea is never under the identified walnut shell, ever. The list of job denials was long and disappointing. Desirable housing was unavailable, so I had to settle for an efficiency apartment in a neighborhood saturated with drugs and sex workers waiting for me to slip on a banana peel and fall back into the life that I had tried to escape. I believed education could help me overcome the stigma of being a convicted felon, even though I would never be able to educate myself enough to not check the box on the application that asks whether I have ever been convicted of a felony. But I could be prepared.

While studying for my BA at the University of the District of Columbia in 2002, I could not vote in the midterm elections because I was on probation in Maryland, Virginia, and DC. While studying for my MFA at Chicago State University from 2004 to 2006, I was prohibited from voting in the presidential elections because not enough time had passed since I had been off probation. In 2008, while studying for my PhD at the State University of New York in Albany, I walked into the voting precinct, gave my name, showed identification, and closed the curtain. It felt like another in a long line of tricks perpetrated by the government, but there I was in a voting booth, and a Black man was on the ballot. The first vote I would ever cast would be for Barack Obama, solely because he was Black. My relationship with the common folk dictated I vote Black; too many of my elders would have jumped out of their caskets and haunted me like an old-time haint until I went mad from terror if I had betrayed the one thing they could feel good about in American life.

There had been my great-great-uncles Bud and Dennis, who, after spending Saturday night in a shot house drinking moonshine and splo, came across the ridge on a Sunday in Guntersville, Alabama, and stumbled upon their cousin Wiley Fennel and his family returning from church in a covered wagon, dust rising from the wooden wheels as they ground against the red dirt. The uncles arrived at the same time as Major King and another, nameless white man, who stopped the wagon and demanded that the women be handed over. What happened next is the family secret that could never be told until the deaths of my great-great-uncles, and is still only mumbled under the breath. Major King and his accomplice's obituaries appeared in the *Democrat*, a week after the encounter, in 1912.

In addition to my great-great-uncles, there had also been my grandfather Big Seventy, or Elvie Horton, a man who couldn't rub two nickels together to make a dime during the Depression.

Big Seventy, relying on the art of cooking moonshine to provide for his wife and soon-to-be-born child, got caught by the revenuers in 1931, went to prison, and missed the birth of his son (my father). Big Seventy worked on the chain gang through convict leasing, was released after a year, and worked thirty years punching iron for the steel plant. Can't forget about Aunt Emma, who migrated from Alabama to the South Side of Chicago, prospered through liquor sales and seamstress work, and paid police and city officials to have her brother released from prison during the day so that he could shine shoes. Yes, I had to carry Wiley, Bud, Dennis, Emma, Big Seventy, Rosie Lee, and the rest of my ancestors into that booth, and there is no way I could look them in the eye and say I was voting for a white man. If I had, I would have lost my Black card in Birmingham, and that is the most precious of cards to own.

No Black person wants to be considered a sellout, a backstabber, a traitor, a recreant turncoat.

While I understood the historicity and that a Black man had a chance to win, the reality did not register until I woke up the next morning with Obama confirmed as the forty-fourth president of the United States. I checked my email and saw a message from a friend in San Diego. That morning he had purchased a flag and hung it on his front porch, and said how proud he was to be an American. Again, with the common folk, there is always a complicated relationship with America. Most of the time it is *fuck America* followed by a litany of reasons explaining why.

If we are totally honest, every culture has certain biases they will never mention outside of the group.

To this very day, I don't know a whole lot of Black folk gushing about America as if they hit the Mega Millions jackpot by being born in this country. They will say things like, *it's cool, dealing with, ain't nobody mad but the folks that ain't getting none, the struggle real, blessed and highly favored, holding on until help come along—and if don't no help come, still holding on*. Comments like this will be part of the American fabric so long as there is a debt to be paid that will never be repaid, so long as the balance of racial power is unequal, so long as there is no more land to be distributed and generational wealth to some is a joke.

Many African Americans are still walking around with that insufficient-funds check in their pocket.

These forgotten citizens are trying to make sense of a nation their ancestors built, damn near from the ground up. The question for my circle of friends has become, How can we be totally proud of a country where there are so many hidden barriers and boundaries in place? My friends want to know why they, as African Americans, always have to lower the head, forgive, and not get? This theme and others like it, stemming from the effects of colonialism in a neocolonial world, undergird discussions by the common folk within Blackness that are often hidden from white America. The fact that the first vote I cast was for a Black person was significant, for until then no one in my family had ever thought it possible for a Black person to be on the ballot. I mean, when I was in grade school and teachers asked us kids what we wanted to be when we grew up, some would say president of the United States, but by the time we reached the age where we had our Baldwin race-realization moment, that hope was not a dream deferred but a dream abandoned.

After reading the email my friend sent, I left my apartment and went to SUNY Albany's campus, where I was within a semester of earning my PhD.

Every African American I encountered that morning seemed to walk a little smoother, with a bop or ideological lean or sway, as if doing some variation of the camel walk, the electric robot, the pop lock, the freak, the dog, or the wop—each chest poked out a little further, each face wearing a Cheshire grin. I was the only African American PhD student in the English department, and in terms of Black professors, there were two. One of them came into the copy room while I was there and gave me the coded look, like *yeah, we did it*. We then gave each other the confirming head nod without uttering a syllable. The conversation flawless in muted translation, confirming we have always been suspicious and untrusting of America. As a matter of fact, I don't know if I've ever said "my country" in a loving and caring context. Don't get me wrong: I understand that I live in a country that offers certain liberties I can't find anywhere else, but the polemical nature of the past is difficult to forget.

My first vote gave me a chance to also bond with my mother, who called me the following night and asked if I would escort her to the inauguration and state dinner.

I would be attending these events courtesy of the National Education Association, which my mother had represented for years as a delegate, traveling to DC to engage in educational policy.

During my former life of unthinkable acts, I never viewed my mother as a trailblazer, yet she was. Part of the first wave of teachers to integrate schools in Jefferson County, she became a central player among educators and rose to become president of the Alabama Education Association. I still have the letters she wrote to me while I was in prison, some enclosed in AEA envelopes, which hinted that although my mother did not really have time to spare, she found the time to stay connected and make sure her son knew that someone in the outside world cared. Many of these envelopes contained small notes of encouragement or indications that she had added a few dollars to what my dad was sending to make sure I could buy the things I needed in commissary.

The state dinner would be a black-tie affair, so I would need a tux, she explained. I looked at this moment as partial atonement for the pain and suffering I caused my mom, the many nights she could not sleep, wondering if I was dead or alive.

During the drive down via the New York State Thruway to the New Jersey Turnpike and then on I-95 to DC, I reflected on the conversations of family and friends obsessed with the image of a Black man as president. The danger of relying on this image was a willingness to make certain concessions regarding Blackness and historical fact and to downplay the sobering reality of race in this country. My fears began when Obama distanced himself from Pastor Jeremiah Wright and his "Goddamn America" speech, which common folk understood perfectly, seeing nothing wrong with telling the truth about a country that had enslaved its lineage for centuries and then wanted a *my bad,* as if to say that it was all in the past and yet refused to address the original sin.

The dominant narrative, however—that is, the white majority—didn't see this conundrum through the same lens. They thought that an apology should suffice, that Wright's damning soliloquy on America was treasonous, an insurrection against the state. How dare Wright criticize a country where Black men are incarcerated at a higher clip than anyone else, where police shootings against unarmed Black men are sanctioned? Not to mention unfair housing practices or the poisoning of communities with toxic waste. Obama left Wright hanging like wet clothes outside on a line, signaling how he would walk the tightrope of race.

Exiting the Capital South Metro station on January 20, 2009, at 8:00 A.M., I became part of the human mass making its way to the mall.

I spent most of my adult life in Washington, DC. I attended the rally on January 15, 1981, to make Martin Luther King Jr.'s birthday a holiday, with Stevie Wonder singing "Happy Birthday" and Jesse Jackson leading the crowd with the chant, "Up with hope, down with dope." Then too, I remember the Million Man March, which I attended on October 16, 1995, while staying in a homeless shelter in Arlington, Virginia. But these two events in consecutive decades paled in comparison to what Obama's election achieved in the new millennium. The streets were congested with people of color in every direction—the intensity in the air so thick you could cut it with a butter knife—every branch of law enforcement revealed by the initials on the back of black windbreakers. On the sidewalks strangers struck up conversations with one another on a whim. I met a Hispanic guy from the Texas Panhandle who traveled to DC to be present for this moment. While we walked down Constitution Avenue, he told me how he felt a new love for the country he lived in.

I did not reveal my apprehensions about his hope, for sometimes hope can be an illusion; I chose not to challenge his moment of faith.

I passed elderly people propped on not one but two canes, pulling and damn near willing themselves toward a narrative in which hope is indeed possible.

Obama had cauterized the racial divide—if only for a moment—and people wanted to see this man make history. My silver-coded ticket enabled me to watch the swearing-in near the Lincoln Memorial Reflecting Pool while my mother watched from a VIP location courtesy of the NEA, complete with catered food and a front-row seat. That was cool by me because my mother didn't need to stand in a crowd thick as molasses. I genuflected, having overcome my own personal tragedies to be present, and understood that my first vote placed me in this moment to represent all those who came before me. Then I stood up, took a deep breath, and looked back at the flow of human bodies past the Washington Monument. Obama's image brought people of all hues together in hopes that we could work out our differences, but this moment in history also brought my mother and me closer.

My mother grew up in a clapboard house surrounded by rows of shotgun houses owned by a parasitic realtor who preyed on the human condition of Black folk in Smithfield.

Her mother, Rosie Lee, operated a shot house, complete with a Rock-Ola jukebox that spun 45s for a dime. Rosie Lee inherited this lot in life from her mother, Mary Davis, before the turn of the twentieth century. My mother came from a lineage of women who operated within the common folk, who understood that illegal activity was the only way to survive a system in the South that not only segregated them by color but refused to see them as human beings. This was supposed to be my mother's inheritance, except Rosie Lee Davis did not want a bootleg life for her only daughter. She called upon an uncle, R.B. McIntosh, who managed to graduate from high school and, because he wanted to be a teacher, decided to go to college.

At the time, R.B. was not allowed to attend an in-state white college that offered the curriculum he wanted, so the good state of Alabama sent him to Northwestern University in Illinois and paid all his expenses.

Alabama paid R.B. to stay away from their ideal of pure whiteness. R.B. became a mentor to my mother, while his niece, Rosie Lee, continued to sell whiskey and rent rooms.

Between these two forces my mother, Eunice Pearl Davis, ended up getting a BA and an MA in education from Alabama A&M University and embarked on a long teaching career. She eventually began working at the AEA, rising to lead the organization as president.

My mother and I attended the Southern States Ball on inauguration night. I could not help but think about all my mother had endured and gained a new appreciation for her accomplishments.

I had disappointed Mom terribly over the years, squandering my potential, living a life no mother could be proud of. I strained our relationship with unacceptable behavior, but with a mother's unyielding love for her offspring, she provided the support I needed to right the ship I wrecked. Now we were both zipping around town, dressed to the nines, attending inauguration gatherings and enjoying the hopeful buzz that ran through DC with kinetic energy. It meant everything in the world to be able to share this moment with the woman who had been the toughest on me when I needed it the most. She refused to condone any of my behavior, and now she was my strongest advocate. I could not help but get caught up in the moment, not for Obama but for my mother and me, as she could see I was becoming the man she envisioned.

I realized this memory would not be about Obama, who would disappoint the common folk because he couldn't be the kind of president we wanted him to be. Every move he made would be calibrated by the implications of race, especially during his first term in office. There would be many criticisms, which would be fair, and although my first ballot ever cast would be for a Black president, the enduring image I am left with from that time is that of being with my mother, the only person who ever came to visit me in county jail, even though she was disheartened.

Washington is a place my mother loves to frequent, yet for all the years I stayed in DC, we never spent time together like we did during the inauguration. I don't know if I will ever again get the feeling I had during that week, but after the festivities were over I knew that my mother and I had formed a better bond. I was becoming a better son, and I loved her so much for birthing me into this world.

Dead Weight

Obtaining a full-time teaching appointment at a college or university is no small feat by itself. Add seven felony convictions, and the barriers could seem insurmountable.

The one-year non-tenure-track position at the University of New Haven was offered after an interview with the chair of the English department, Don Smith, and another department faculty member. While on the phone, Smith probably thought I gave zero flying fucks about employment, with my deafening silence and unwillingness to be as excited as he was about the offer. I wanted him to somehow understand that the inexplicable silence belonged to former inmate 289-128. Since he could not read tea leaves or tarot cards, I wondered what protocol to follow in admitting to seven felonies and outlining the narrative of their occurrence when trying to gain productive employment. How does a person negotiate the dead weight that attaches itself to the body after being discharged from prison?

Explaining seven felonies to the person holding the fate of your livelihood in their palm is like flossing alligator teeth.

On the surface, having seven felony convictions suggests a lifelong dedication to criminal activity. According to stereotype, felons are committed to wrongdoing, so their chances for contributing to the hypocritical society that asserts *debt paid* are minimal. Before incarceration I had minor brushes with the law—shoplifting, misdemeanor obstruction of justice, destruction of property, unlawful entry, trespassing, possession, and possession with intent to distribute—but none of these led to prison time.

My felony convictions stemmed from two court cases, one in Virginia and the other in Maryland, over three years, beginning in 1997. In the first case, I served an eighteen-month sentence for three felony theft convictions to run concurrent with a six-month misdemeanor sentence. In the second case, I was convicted of three felony counts of theft by possession along with one felony count of second-degree burglary, the latter being classified as violent even though no violence or threat of violence took place. I was sentenced to five years at Roxbury; after serving a year I was transferred to a drug rehabilitation program at a facility in Durham, North Carolina, and released in 2000.

The situation is complicated, and the offenses were not lifelong, but there will forever be the dead weight of seven felony convictions. The number seven usually symbolizes some form of good luck, like three sevens making blackjack with the dealer holding twenty; in Chinese culture, however, seven is symbolic of death. In order to kill the memory, you have to relive it. It's really at that moment, and we all have one, where the thought of outrunning history becomes fantasy.

No matter how hard you churn both legs, or how evenly the hands and elbows slice the wind while getting ghost—dead weight and prison ID 289-128 catch up with you.

One felony is a memory refusing to die. Seven could be considered an eternal nightmare. I gave a truncated explanation to Smith, the department chair, first by phone and then in person. From his office I went directly to Ron Nowaczyk, the dean of arts and sciences, to regurgitate my state of affairs. Nowaczyk remained indifferent during my presentation, and I didn't know if he believed me or was preparing to throw me out of his office. When I was done he asked, "Is that it?" and matter-of-factly pointed me to the human resources department, where I would repeat the process and prepare for the background check to confirm what I'd already revealed. At the time, I was living in Albany, having completed a PhD in English and creative writing in May 2009, and when I returned home, I kept waiting for the phone to ring and a voice telling me that there was no way in hell I would be working at the University of New Haven. When the phone did ring, however, I was informed by the administration that all the information I provided was confirmed by the background check. I would be allowed to teach during the upcoming school year.

Because it was only a one-year appointment, I did not know where I would be teaching afterward. So, during that first semester, while preparing lesson plans and syllabi, meeting students during office hours, and teaching classes, I applied for several jobs elsewhere in the country.

In November, I received a call from David Shevin, the chair of Central State University's English department, informing me that out of about two hundred applications, mine had been selected for the Distinguished Scholar-in-Residence post. I would be responsible for three tasks during the spring semester: (1) teaching an honors class on culture memory, trauma, and the Black radical tradition; (2) delivering a campus-wide lecture on poetics; and (3) giving a poetry reading in the community. The residency came with a stipend of thirty thousand dollars, and I accepted it.

When I told Smith about the job offer, he immediately went to Nowaczyk to see if my position could be held until I got back, practically guaranteeing that I would work at UNH well past my one-year appointment. The decision to leave was difficult since the institution had blind faith in my ability to do the job, motivate students, and provide them with a learning experience to prepare them for what lay ahead outside the university walls. But the opportunity to teach at a historically Black university was something I couldn't pass up, given how I had squandered my undergraduate years at Howard University in Washington, DC. Only a few years earlier, Howard had introduced me to the dead weight when it denied my reentry to the university upon my release from prison.

Central State mailed me the contract, and I returned it, signed, within forty-eight hours.

Three weeks after my initial conversation with Smith, after having told him I would not be back for the spring semester, I received a registered letter from the provost of Central State, which basically stated, *Dr. Horton, after careful reconsideration of our initial offer, as provost of Central State University I am rescinding our offer based on discrepancies in your application. Please do not call or attempt to contact us.* Shevin, the chair of Central State's English department, called me later that night, furious at the university's decision. The provost had told Shevin not to contact me, but out of sheer morality and humanness, he did reach out to let me know what really went down.

I had fully disclosed my past when I applied for the position and when I accepted the offer over the phone. Shevin assured me it would present no problem whatsoever. I didn't hide the minor brushes with the law or the felony theft, second-degree burglary, or theft by possession charges. I was upfront about all of it. I'd admitted to being a drug smuggler, drug seller, and drug addict. At that point in my life, a Google search of

"Randall Horton" would have produced screen after screen of negative information about my past. It was something I could never outrun, so I ran straight toward it, placing the dead-weight narrative in my own hands instead of someone else's.

On the phone Shevin went into great detail about how the provost seemed hell-bent on not having an ex-felon on campus.

Subsequently, Shevin hired a lawyer on his own dime to see if the revocation could be reversed. After talking with me and agreeing that Central State's actions were uncalled for, the lawyer met with the university's general counsel and was told that Central State officials did not care if I sued for breach of contract. They were willing to go to court and lose rather than have my ex-convict self working at their long-standing institution that focused on the betterment of African Americans. The lawyer told me that I did have a case and would likely win, but I would need to weigh the pros and cons of filing suit.

For one thing, because I had one more semester on my contract at New Haven, any damages I would receive would be offset by potential earnings, meaning I would get only twenty thousand dollars minus the attorney's fee. Second, and more important, if I sued Central State, I would be put on a blacklist, and it would become harder for me to get a job in academia.

Central State's defiance and intimidation left me pondering the actual purpose of an HBCU. The situation brought me back to Amiri Baraka's autobiography and his recollections of life at Howard University in the 1950s. One day a faculty member witnessed him eating watermelon while sitting on the school's wall facing Georgia Avenue—a main artery of traffic within Washington, DC—and told him he was setting Negroes back fifty years. Baraka would constantly question why Black institutions tried to "outwhite the whites," arguing that these *knew-knee-grows* seemed stuck in the age of the New Negro, measuring all accomplishments against the success and prestige of white institutions.

After the dust settles, or when the ashes clear, what path lies before the social outcast who carries the dead weight of prison? Is redemption possible within the community the outcast came from?

It is important for these communities and social networks to realize that, according to a 2020 report by the Pew Research Center, Blacks are "far more likely" to be incarcerated than Hispanics and whites. At the end of 2018, the study found, Blacks were imprisoned at a rate nearly twice that of Hispanics and more than five times that of whites. When you think about the incarceration rate for African Americans, how the prison-industrial complex attaches itself through parole, probation, and conviction long after release, you would expect HBCUs to be at the forefront of reeducation and rehabilitation. This was not the position, however, that Central State was taking with its decision. I would have loved to have sat down and talked with the provost, but I never got the chance. I would have told the provost that I am the product of an HBCU union, my mother and father having met at Alabama A&M University. But more than that, I would have explained how my parents' love for HBCUs filtered down to my sister and me. They made sure that we attended the Magic City Classic, a game between the oldest HBCU football rivals in the country, Alabama A&M and Alabama State University. My sister graduated from A&M, her oldest daughter is an alumna too, and her youngest is on track to finish in two years. My parents' friends attended HBCUs as well.

I would have told the provost how I made a series of mistakes for which I have deep remorse, but since my release I have been doing everything in my power to make sure I contribute positively not only to the Black experience but to the human experience. Again, however, I never got the chance to prove that I was indeed worthy of having been picked by Central State's English students and seconded by the faculty to be a Distinguished Fellow even though they all knew my incarceration history. Instead, Central State administrators chose to add to the dead weight one carries after prison, reinforcing stereotypes while being contradictory and hypocritical in carrying out its mission. True, the university owed me nothing; and yet, I did not ask for a handout—only to be judged on merit and the ability to have an impact on campus.

That rejection brought me back to the first one at Howard University, which I now realize was the first sign of the residue of incarceration that would never go away.

When I tried to reenroll at Howard after my release from prison, I believed that my being a returning student, along with well-documented rehabilitation, would result in an acceptance letter. The letter I received, however, was very different, announcing the rejection of my application because of my felony convictions. This news destroyed the dream I had dreamt every night in cell 23: to get an undergraduate degree from Howard University, to finish what I started, to prove I could represent the university in a positive manner. I wanted to prove that I had changed but was not given the opportunity by the Black elite at Howard. Instead I went to the University of the District of Columbia, which accepted me unconditionally.

Given my disappointment with HBCUs, it was both a surprise and an honor to be invited in 2018 to deliver the annual Ralph Ellison Lecture at Tuskegee University in southeast Alabama. The HBCU, located about sixty-five miles from my hometown of Birmingham, was home to the likes of Booker T. Washington and George Washington Carver. Ellison attended the university and wrote the great postmodern novel *Invisible Man*, whose protagonist gets immersed in a brand of Blackness that is not only confusing but terrifying. The irony of my selection to deliver the address on Tuskegee's pristine campus, with its rich Black history, did not escape me. I could not help but think, *Who knows but that, on the lower frequencies, I speak for you?* as I began to address a room of hopeful college students. Perhaps the time is now to publicly question HBCU institutions like Howard and Central State that adopt the same philosophies the protagonist in *Invisible Man* had to endure at the mythical HBCU in Ellison's novel—a philosophy that mimicked the mentality of the oppressor to further oppress those who blindly subscribed to operating within the white gaze.

I am left with the terrible realization that the institutions I love so much are helping to perpetuate a troubling brand of Blackness.

The University of New Haven is not a large institution, so I'm not exactly operating with a lot of research money or summer stipends, but I have been resourceful, and my experience there has been great. After that first year I went on the job market again, but I also applied for and received a tenure-track position at UNH, and was awarded tenure after five years. I am the only person of color in my department, but when I teach courses that educate students about Blackness, enrollment is always at capacity, with the majority being students of color. Also, I never lose sight of the fact that many of the students I cross paths with will be employed in some form of criminal justice, which is the reason many attend this university. I am the unicorn, the outlier my students need to see before they pursue their chosen profession. It is my hope that these future leaders will remember Dr. Horton—what he stood for and how he tried to exemplify change and dispel stereotypes and misconceptions about convicted felons.

My office is in need of a coat of paint, and its thirty-year-old industrial rug has only recently been replaced—slow change, but change. The wall is gradually being filled with framed photos of memorable events and occasions.

Years have passed since Central State rescinded its offer of employment. After teaching two classes on a Monday, I slide back into my chair and turn on the desktop. I log onto Facebook, where I see a post reporting that David Shevin has passed away. I am stunned. Shevin was the chair of the English department at Central State. He saw the real me on a curriculum vitae that offered no human connection; and yet, the people Shevin interacted with on a daily basis refused to see me for who I was or what I could become. Shevin believed in me so much, he hired counsel to fight my cause—placed his job and livelihood in jeopardy so that I might have a chance. Through this guy I was able to see the good in humanity. Shevin died with no one knowing this part of him but me.

Imagine if more human beings like Shevin looked beneath the surface to see the prison-industrial complex for the damage it does? We have to remember that the original mandate of HBCUs was to provide an opportunity for African Americans coming out of slavery, not only to help them be competitive in a capitalistic society but to level the playing field. If we are to believe author Michelle Alexander's assertion that mass incarceration is the new Jim Crow, then what mechanisms are in place to assist those caught in this new systemic bias against Black people and people of color? And yes, shame on Howard, Central State, and the many other HBCUs whose policies sometimes outwhite the whites instead of helping the community they swore to protect and serve.

Perception versus Reality

It is 1992. Full-blown gentrification is at least ten years away and will erase all evidence that we occupied this space.

But for now, my friends and business partners Dirty Red, Big Foots, Dee, and I are huddled in a crevice between storefronts on Park Road, selling dimes and twenties of cocaine. Like-minded entrepreneurs operate nearby along with the addicted and the homeless, giving license to the term "open air market," meaning, cash and carry—and smoke all you can as long as you can. Sharing this subjugated space is a car hanging a right onto Park Road in what looks like slow motion. My eyes register the turning car at barely two miles per hour before it comes to a complete stop in the middle of the street. A man hops out of the passenger side at a rate of speed that will feel much faster when I rewind the scenario years later, but for an instant, the man could be treading through five feet of liquid tar. There is a Glock at his side as he maneuvers between two parked cars, steps into our personal space, then places the tip of the gun barrel on the scalp of the person who is bending down alongside Dee and trying to decide which dime he will choose from those in the bag. At the moment of the gun's contact with his scalp, the customer who is stooped with Dee realizes that a bullet is milliseconds away from tunneling into his brain and ducks—causing the now-fired bullet to slightly graze his skull. This minor gesture alters the bullet's trajectory enough that it tears through blue jeans and cotton underwear and explodes Dee's left testicle. Dee is now lying in a pool of blood on the pavement minus a left testicle while the gunman retraces his steps back to the waiting car. The intended target, meanwhile, flees east on Park Road. Realizing that Dee could die from the gunshot wound, Big Foots, all six-foot-seven of him, scoops Dee up off the pavement, carrying him like a rag doll to my Samurai parked down the street. We drive down Irving Street, cross over to Park Place, and merge onto Michigan Avenue all the way to Washington Hospital.

We carry Dee through the emergency entrance doors, looking like we had come from a military combat zone with blood on our clothes and were entering a triage unit.

Past events, scenes with rising and falling action that refuse erasure by the passage of time, often resurface while I am addressing a classroom full of undergraduate students who trust me as a symbol of authority and expertise. How ironic the situation, especially at an institution that specializes in keeping the prison-industrial complex supplied with young people who are fascinated by the forensics and crime scene investigation portrayed in TV crime shows. The programming they've watched builds a brand off criminality and incarceration, reinforcing a criminal justice system that criminalizes the perceived criminal long before contact. Until my class, these students had never been taught by a professor with seven felony convictions. So, when I appear in flesh and bone as a palpable human being with stories to recapitulate what they thought they knew into what should be known, the students are indeed curious about their perception versus my reality. Their knowledge of incarceration, the criminal justice system, and what occurs while one is detained is riddled with stereotypes, misbeliefs, misconceptions, generalities, or plain naïveté. In most of my introductory classes, I have my students read the award-winning play *Short Eyes*, by Nuyorican poet and former Sing Sing resident Miguel Piñero, whose characters offer the reader an unflinching narrative of what really occurs on the inside.

The prison in the play, based on Rikers Island, is emblematic of an inverted society where the Black and Latino population dominates the narrative, settling disputes and keeping social order. Whiteness is at their mercy, there being no privilege enjoyed by white detainees. One Latino inmate, named Cupcakes, realizes quickly that he is not as street tough as he imagined and becomes prey to sexual predators much more callous and desensitized to humanity. He is constantly subjected to unwanted sexual advances by Blacks and Latinos and realizes that there is no refuge for the weak and feeble. Race alone cannot save Cupcakes from potentially being deflowered.

This is the point in the play where my students and I usually need to have a conversation about prison rape. Many of them think that Piñero's play exaggerates the prevalence of sexual assault, believing the narrative they've been taught over the years that downplays the existence of prison rape. One student, who later follows in his father's footsteps to become a correctional officer, remains adamant that rape does not happen in prison anymore.

This is what I tell them: in Housing Unit III, C-Tier, of Roxbury Correctional Institution, when someone is escorted out of his cell with all of his belongings, it is often because some form of sexual assault has been happening in the cell.

Deboe, my first cellie, was in for murder, walking down a sixty-year stretch. Across the hall, Tony, who was serving three years for distributing drugs, came and asked whether I would switch cells with him, if the correctional officer approved. His cellie was Big Pun, who was closer to my own age, so I figured that young'uns wanted to be with young'uns and went along with the request, no harm, no foul. Deboe and Tony, who were both from Southeast DC, were inseparable after that day—sold commissary together, hung out in the yard, acted tough—and some guys were afraid of them. One day about six months after that cell move, the extended time for evening lock-in signaled that something was wrong.

A cell door rolled back, and Tony was escorted out by correctional officers, his possessions in a cardboard box and his head covered with a wool blanket. As each of us, our faces pressed against the rectangular glass windows of our cell doors, watched Tony walk down the hall, we knew that he had checked in to protective custody. Deboe was raping Tony in the cell where Deboe and I had once sat up late at night, talking about what we used to do on the streets. After the other cell doors opened back up, news circulated quickly.

I have given each student something to ponder. Nobody looks me directly in the eye. The truth can be uncomfortable, so I ease up a bit.

The correctional officer's son believed that his father was a good guy, and perhaps he was. The student confided to me that he admired my resiliency, how I escaped my environment to teach at the university level. Over time our relationship morphed into mentor and mentee, and I decided to tell him about a correctional officer I knew named Big Grip.

Before serving my sentence at Roxbury, I was housed at Seven Locks in a unit dedicated to rehabilitation and alternatives to incarceration. Big Grip's shift usually lasted until evening lock-in. Over the course of eight months in the block, I was allowed to leave my cell during lock-in to clean the unit and prepare meal trays for the other inmates. Standing six-foot-nine and weighing close to three hundred pounds, Big Grip was the antithesis of most correctional officers I came in contact with during my time on the inside.

I started talking with Big Grip about growing up in the South and about the racism we both endured as children of the '60s. He played basketball at a small Division II school in the Midwest, so we talked a lot about sports too. What's more important about the conversations is that we talked human to human. Big Grip didn't talk down to me or treat me like a plebe. I came to understand that as a correctional officer he was not the norm—that he was as different from normal as they came.

The first time I returned to the inside without *guilty* and *sentenced to* attached to my name was at Seven Locks, where I was asked to come and talk about my journey from prison to PhD. Upon entering, I wondered whether I had gone insane or somehow developed amnesia. Here were the same halls I once walked, hands cuffed behind my back, the blue trumpeted melodies still hidden but screaming within the walls; where my one and only visitor was my mother, who traveled all the way from Birmingham, Alabama, to Montgomery County, Maryland, wanting to see her only son; where I learned that girlfriends leave the bad guys once they are locked up, that friends disappear, and that the family you thought you had on the street was not your family. On my first night inside a fistfight occurred, and I discovered the importance of keeping shoes on at all times to avoid slipping and falling on the concrete floor while engaged in a physical altercation. I learned this valuable lesson by observing my cellmate throw hands with a dude over a word exchange, and because the other dude did not have sneakers on and my cellie did, victory was determined by shoe traction.

Blood splattered on the concrete floor all the way to my cell door, and *ain't nobody see nothing* is what we told the guards to protect my cellmate from solitary confinement and the dreaded hole. When I left to go upstate, Big Grip said he didn't want to see me again, but when he did see me again and I wasn't wearing a jumpsuit with an inmate number, Big Grip gave me a tight hug, like he was proud of what I had become, as if he always knew. That day I sat in the same circle I once sat in and shared my essays and poems on my changing self, except that this time I led the discussions. We talked about what it was like to reenter society with the mark of *ex-convict*, and the road that would have to be traveled to participate in the great American experiment.

I gave the guys what I could, what worked for me; yet I know it wasn't enough, because I left and they stayed behind.

I tell my students that guys on the inside often have nicknames like *Woke, Baby-Cy, Frog, Bluemeat, Graveyard Pimp, Chicken Head, Knuck, Pappy, Cat, Wolf, Butterbean, Milkman, Blacker-Than-Me, Hot-Rod, Germ, Neck-Bone, Rat-Killa, Nose, Wine, Hell-Naw, Blade, Uzi, Grapeball, Fat-Man, Heist, Lil Nine, Folks, Big Foots, White-Boy, Cuban,* and *Disco*—names that give them an identity in a society that fails to fully recognize their presence. Many of these men use deviancy as a form of rebellion against a system that has not pledged allegiance to them, a system that perpetuates racism and other forms of oppression. The men also carry other names, like *felon, convict, inmate,* and *prisoner*—names that will never leave them once they are released (if they are lucky) into the world. These guys will always be an *ex* something, fighting a stereotype that hovers like an albatross over anyone connected to the criminal justice system, whether past or present, even me. I tell my students that not a single person will go to jail for not being a nice person. It isn't illegal to be rotten, to be an adulterer, to keep cultures in poverty through legal practices, or to harbor hatred for people. My students know this, yet fail to make the correlations.

A funeral or homegoing for my identity as *ex* has been in the making for quite some time.

I can honestly say this now, without regret, without worrying that someone might not understand its necessity. The death of nomenclature such as *felon, convict, inmate, prisoner,* and *ex* within the language of reform must occur if criminal justice is to evolve. For society to advance and rethink how it addresses those entangled in the criminal justice system, the language it uses must also be reevaluated. I've been calling myself *ex-felon, ex-convict, ex-inmate,* and *ex-prisoner* because, as an advocate, a real-life example works better than a hypothesis. Those skeptical of radical reform want me to retell my transgressions in great detail, using a restrictive language I neither wish to use nor believe in. Above all else, they want to be convinced that I am morally good now, that I am full of redeemable qualities. I need to share stories like the Park Road incident, with its violence and guns, because they reinforce the tropes the skeptics expect to hear and process. I need to reassure them that I am not that person anymore.

The performance of myself as ex-convict, someone with seven felony convictions who manages to overcome these hurdles, seems great and awe inspiring on the surface.

I say *performance* because I know I am not an ex-anything. It took time, but I eventually realized that my thinking was a setup, the way the narrative was supposed to be, that even my greatest achievements would echo and reaffirm the system. The con is actually the system itself—manipulating language to denote deviant behavior. *Ex* as a label plays tricks on people returning to society by making them unsure of their self-worth. They are duped into believing that to achieve social normalcy, their repentance must always be juxtaposed against the mark, the stain, or the felony that is more of a cattle brand, a signage of identification and ownership; thus, any advancement comes at the expense of the self and celebrates the system that contained that self.

Ultimately, the question becomes, How can one ever be unblemished with such a stain?

For example, after serving a prison bid and rehabilitation program, I found it terrifying to sit with a roomful of strangers at the University of the District of Columbia, though one could say I should have felt lucky to be in a college classroom. Early on, I constantly felt judged as I took notes, as though no matter how hard I tried to hide the mark of the *ex*, people knew and were criticizing me behind my back, labeling me as something bad, even if I tried to represent good. I wasn't that dude on Park Road anymore, but they didn't care. I could sense the interior dialogue: *Did you hear about the dude in your class who has been locked up? Keep an eye on him, he might steal something.*

The obligation to explain those felony convictions became dehumanizing to the point that I would get angry at people who inquired about my past—as if their house stood spotless, as if something from their childhood or college days or some other dastardly moment in time that had been suppressed was not real; and yet, it was I who was regularly put on the witness stand to explain myself. I needed to be humble to a fault, careful to straddle the line between confident and arrogant.

I struggled to find value in this new self, independent of the *ex* that I was trying to create.

Then there were the dinner parties and get-togethers with upwardly mobile people who presented the illusion that their lives were perfect, that they were morally good and had never done a wrong thing, that it was I, the *ex*, who didn't quite fit the mold.

Questions like *What do you do? Where did you go to school? What are you working on now? What career path did you take?* often created a deer-in-the-headlights moment for me—they all ultimately led back to the inside. The best piece of advice I received after my release came from Big Fred, an old hustling buddy, who was very familiar with a cell.

Big Fred had completed a two-year federal bid and was working as a real estate and mortgage lender in Washington, DC. One night, after a cookout at his house, we talked about the weight one carries after prison. Big Fred told me that everybody has a little clutter in the closet, that the people you think are doing okay are at times living in their own form of hell. He went through a list of men and women we knew who lacked felony convictions but were known to be evil, rotten, nasty, and malicious, yet society treated them as if they were angels, incapable of doing a wrong thing, ever. This imbalance in moral judgment is why the *ex* must die.

I'm not going to chase my own tail, nor will I continue to use language from the handler's toolbox to deconstruct and define my own existence.

Why strengthen criminology's image as guardian through my personal narrative? I prefer to create my own toolbox of language. So, to the person who carried that old toolbox: the death of *ex* will not be caused by the blade, a slash across the wrist or throat, bleeding out in night silence. It will not be caused by an entry and exit wound, torn flesh, or bullet to the temple that splatters bone and brain matter. This death will be effected by a brushstroke across the canvas of life, blotting out the current image to get to a more viable image in the eye of the beholder. My goal is to erase a stereotypical life drawn without permission, correcting a wrong for the sake of a right, or righteousness. This death I seek will be done by erasure.

Can Poetry Save a Life?

for the poet Derek A. Anderson

William Carlos Williams wrote this well-known verse in "Asphodel, That Greeny Flower":

> It is difficult
> to get the news from poems
> yet men die miserably every day
> for lack
> of what is found there.

In 1998, I did not know this poem or the fact that William Carlos Williams ever existed—but to be fair, I didn't know any poems or poets when I entered Seven Locks in Montgomery County, Maryland, facing a slew of felony charges. I was held in this county jail for more than a year, trying to resolve the numerous cases against me before I would take a plea deal and be shackled and shipped on a Bluebird bus to Roxbury Correctional Institution, the state penitentiary. Three months before my sentencing date, on a whim, I decided to escape the boredom of routine and sign up for a poetry workshop offered by a volunteer group of writers from New York City. I didn't really expect anything from the experience other than getting out of the block for a couple of hours. I mean, I was reading and writing prose to pass the time in my jail cell, but poetry was an outlier, something not on my radar. I had never attended a workshop of any kind, except in 1981 in a dorm room at Howard University, when my man Dukes, who was from Miami, showed a group of young entrepreneurs how to cook powder cocaine into freebase rock.

Two poems introduced to us during the first workshop would eventually send me on a journey that I am still traveling. We read

"Autobiography in Five Short Chapters" by Portia Nelson, a five-part poem about the paths human beings choose in life, particularly how we go down the same path repeatedly, only to realize that it is a dead end. The other poem, "Find Your Own Voice" by Jayne Cortez, was about the power of the pen and language. In one section she writes, "so I tell you whoever you are / plastic pen, paper dictionary." These words resonated with us in the workshop, as we each held jail-issued plastic pens, white legal pads, and a small dictionary. I managed to save the workshop handouts, and although I no longer have the poems I wrote at the time, I still carry the feeling of achievement, of being able to see past the physical bars that tried to define who and what I could become through poetry. I did not have to be other people's definition of society's expectations. I left the workshop understanding that poetry could perhaps save my life, if I gave it a chance.

In 2007, during a reading with poets Cara Benson and Carol Graser at a poetry series in Albany, New York, I read a sequence of poems on the time I spent at Roxbury. After the event, Cara invited me to visit her creative writing class at Mt. McGregor Correctional Facility, about an hour north of Albany. Turns out, Cara started the program in 2006 to fulfill a teaching requirement and kept it going on a voluntary basis. She thought I would be a perfect fit for her students. Before attending the workshop, I was invited to participate in a poetry reading series at the prison, held twice a month in the chapel. Cara drove us there, negotiating the snaky roads slick with snow and ice while I took note of the wild turkeys and deer dotting the way to the facility, which sat on top of a mountain. After arriving, I went through security—emptying my pockets, getting the wand passed over my body, and observing the suspicious looks by guards as they thumbed through books of mine that they would never read.

The series was hosted by an inside person, Sean Dalpiaz, who would become a close friend after his release. The event was one of the most powerful readings I've witnessed. To see these guys confidently walk to the podium, read their crafted poems, and receive handclaps and cheers, holding on to the hope that poetry gave them, was something that not only burned a fire inside my chest but also gave me hope.

During my time working with the guys at the Mt. McGregor workshop, it became clear that poetry, or the news from poetry, along with the news in their poems, was a form of rehabilitation and reconciliation with the past and the promise of a future. We didn't talk much about incarceration poems or poems by those once on the inside, like Etheridge Knight, Jimmy Santiago Baca, or Ricardo Sanchez, though the guys loved and were very familiar with their work. The men were more interested in poems that took them outside of their physical and mental location, and often their poems reflected this thought process. Many stood out as capable poets who could make an impact on the current literary landscape.

Sean Dalpiaz, Derek A. Anderson, Celestial, Coda, and Melvin Williams were participants I would never forget. That said, Coda was the one whose poetry could have been published right then because of the way he described himself in relation to the world he had known. Coda's craft and his attention to fine poetic details were amazing, and he could transcend the cage that held him, effortlessly. Unfortunately, Coda remains locked in a system that may never give him a second chance.

Not too long ago, Sean celebrated his fortieth birthday and invited my wife and me to his party. Since his release in 2013, he has integrated back into society, making a positive impact in many ways. I can also say the same for Celestial and Melvin. During Sean's birthday party in Long Island, memories of our poetry workshop at Mt. McGregor flooded my brain, and I began to understand what William Carlos Williams was getting at in that often-quoted passage in "Asphodel." But I also wondered what was so special about this workshop. What was it about poetry that saved these men's lives and set them on a positive path?

Derek is no longer with us; he passed away unexpectedly almost two years after his release. He did the most time of all of us, and I had new respect for him when I learned that he could have been released years earlier if only he had told the parole board what they wanted to hear, that he was guilty of his crime. Instead, Derek maintained his innocence at each hearing, even when the prospect of freedom hovered so near.

Derek's resilience came to mind as I sought to understand the value of poetry as redemption. I reached out to his widow, Marcella Anderson, who was his rock while he was alive. Wanting to honor Derek's memory in some small way, I asked Marcella a series of questions about him that only someone who was close to him could have answered.

RH: What was it about poetry that helped Derek survive his time on the inside?

MA: Derek explained that at first it was just a way to clear his mind and help with the injustice that had been done to him. Reading his own words gave him a sense of power and peace, a reminder that his mind was still sharp and capable of processing thoughts and feelings. Derek said he used poetry as a way to stay in a hole when his survival instincts were suggesting he become an animal, so to speak. Being in such a harsh environment, eventually Derek succumbed to those animal instincts and walked away from writing for a while, but not completely. Derek said he would have random thoughts and write them down on several different pieces of paper each day over several months, then eventually, clarity would come back and he would gather all the pieces of paper he had written on, resulting in a few amazing poems. Through poetry, Derek found a new sense of purpose, which resulted in a few pieces being published in *Ebony* magazine. Poetry made survival possible. Derek survived and walked with pride!

RH: Many of the guys that came out of that group came home to lead productive lives, including Derek. What was it about poetry that helped him in that ever-changing process?

MA: Coming home after thirty-one years, poetry allowed for a place where Derek could put his anger and bitterness to rest while allowing him to look past the stares and wonder of inquiring minds, and that he did survive! Poetry helped him stay centered and grounded. Derek would tell me in life there are social classes; however, poetry removes all traces of class. Having a poet's mind allowed Derek to see, feel, and ultimately present himself with dignity, which he conveyed to other people when they tried to judge him for having been incarcerated. Derek also would often tell me that poetry can hypnotize the harshest of critics, and this allowed him to thrive in environments that saw him as a felon. Poetry let him live under the radar of judgment and scrutiny and allowed him to be seen and heard and not judged.

RH: What was the most memorable thing about Derek's poetry workshop on the inside?

MA: Derek would tell me that it was being around like-minded people, and feeling a sense of camaraderie that he loved the most about the workshops. The workshop became a place where hope was truly alive. Derek told me that he would always feel like a child on Christmas morning while waiting for the guys to check over his new poem and give him feedback. When the workshop instructor referred to him as "Derek Anderson, the poet," he felt like King Kong and at that point, he realized the sky was the limit, even if he would have to be behind the walls for the rest of his life. Derek was going to make sure he touched someone's life the way this poetry workshop had touched his. When Derek was released and able to share the stage with his poetry instructors, he told me that was one of the best feelings ever.

Change, Changed, or Changing?

Admitting to seven felony convictions in a roomful of people often creates a pause between one thought and the next—a sudden hesitation. Seven felonies means one felony away from habitual-offender status, which carries a life sentence in prison. The fear of one wrong decision is real; it never relinquishes its hold on the day-to-day life of returning citizens, no matter how many degrees they acquire. This is what I assert to the young people I am talking to at the Tennessee Valley Juvenile Detention Center, in the northwest corner of Alabama. I tell them about my mistakes, the memories I am not proud of, the bad decisions I wish I could erase but can't. What I do not tell them about is the incident from the day before, during the journey from New York City to Birmingham via Dallas.

Long-distance travel tends to produce an insatiable hunger in me, so after my plane landed at Dallas–Fort Worth International Airport, I found the connecting gate, took note of the time, and dashed over to Whataburger for a bite to eat.

Here is where life gets unpredictable, where those unexpected flukes, that out-of-the-blue bullshit, really creates a post-traumatic-stress-disorder moment. One wrong choice could spell the difference between lockup and freedom—being in solitary confinement doing pushups and sit-ups versus being at the crib fiddling with the remote. It's a split-second decision, but it doesn't concern the food I'm ordering at Whataburger or the people in line waiting for their order number to be called so that they can eat. It's really about the white man with *racist* printed all over his T-shirt. That word is not visible, of course; only GROOM appears on the shirt, indicating that he just got married, but I know the type, spent the first eighteen years of my life dealing with that kind of individual on a regular basis in Birmingham. I can see bullshit coming before it hits the fan, which most Southern racists don't mind letting fly.

Here's the scene: the white man received his order but didn't get the requisite napkins and straws, which were stored in an area behind the Black female cashier. Evidently he believed that white privilege exempted him from the rules of common courtesy, so rather than request the items or ask whether he could get them himself, he simply meandered behind the counter, grabbed a handful of napkins and straws, and casually saun- tered back, acting like it was okay except that it was not. The cashier reminded him, in a civil manner, "Sir, you are not allowed to do that." This comment infuriated the white man, who was astonished at the audacity of a Black woman telling him how to behave in public. He fired back with racist and misogynistic epithets, calling her a female dog. This guy was a two-fer: a racist and a misogynist. Doesn't get better than that. He then huffed and hurled a wad of napkins in the cashier's face. Let me repeat: he huffed and hurled a wad of napkins in the cashier's face. Now the white man felt empowered because all the other whites in line were looking around stupidly, as though a big-ass elephant had taken a crap in the living room and nobody smelled it.

I smelled the crap strong, standing in line behind the white man. So strong I could not breathe, the stench choking me to death.

Here is what the guy didn't know: I'm thinking about the day I decided to change, to become a responsible world citizen, one commit- ted to making sound decisions while treating people as human beings. I had never met the cashier before, but I knew her, been knowing her for years, though I couldn't tell you her name from Eve. She was a composite of all the Black women I have known. She could have been my grandma's friend Sledge, who worked at Deluxe Beauty Shop as a beautician and therapist for all the ladies whose problems she heard about while doing their hair. She could have been Dot, who worked part time at the clapboard juke joint my grandma ran, pouring shots of cheap gin. She could even have been my grandma, Rosie Lee Davis, who paid off the Birmingham police for the privilege of operating a juke joint in the '50s, '60s, '70s, and early '80s.

The cashier must have needed that job at Whataburger or else she would have snatched a Mississippi knothole in that white man's ass, of that I am certain.

She wanted to cry so badly she convulsed, her chest rising and fall- ing. When she looked around in search of empathy, we briefly made eye contact, and I grasped her situation. Losing this job would mean unemployment and a precarious financial situation—dealing with the electric bill that had come due, the disconnection notice for the cable, the insurance and burial premiums that were a month behind, the grand-kids' cell phone service that might be cut off. The cashier had bills that one paycheck would never cover. This was my assessment at a glance. And no, the belligerent white man didn't know the exploits of Hook, that persona long ago discarded when I walked out of prison and vowed to start a new life. Hook would have coldcocked the joker—damn the consequences. Square to the temple is how I drew it up in my head, calculating how much space I'd need to wind back, how much weight to apply to the left leg as I led with an overhanded right hook. The next day, the headline in the *Dallas Morning News* would read, WHITE MALE KNOCKED INTO THE MIDDLE OF NEXT WEEK FOR DISRESPECTING BLACK LADY AT DFW. But I knew that if I swung the way I imagined, I would be back in prison serving a life sentence, and I didn't need imagination to re-create that setting.

Change is difficult, arduous, complicated, awkward, and, above all else, a verb. You cannot wish your way into instigating change or hope that it descends from the sky, knocking you upside the head. Change demands action, that you do something to alter your current state of being in favor of another. Change is knowing that you cannot talk to a group of kids about change if you, yourself, have not changed.

I am the controller of my narrative, so at the airport I decided to seek the assistance of 5-O, Johnny-Jump-Out, the po-po, the Feds, the Boys in Blue. Spent my whole life running from the semblance of authority, and at this moment of crisis, at a fork in the road, I walked over to a group of uniformed officers at a service desk not far from this flashpoint. There was no other way to deal with the situation if I wanted change.

I did not share this troubling memory with the kids, but they were still primed for empathy, so I let them know in other ways that I was, indeed, one of them.

When I recall the hours I spent standing on a corner under a lamp-light to sell thirty dime bags made from three-and-a-half grams of crack, their heads pop to attention. I rhetorically ask, Have you ever ridden shotgun in a speedboat across the Atlantic, fleeing drug enforcement officials while carrying five hundred kilos of cocaine starboard and port-side? Or strolled through US Customs at Miami International Airport with a mule carrying four kilos of cocaine? Admitting to breaking down a kilo into small amounts for street distribution might not be the way to begin a conversation, but truth knows no starting point: it is what it is. I also describe what it's like being held at gunpoint on the Florida Turnpike because of a drug deal gone awry, and what that means in terms of mortality.

I tell them that there is no upside to this way of living, that a felony has no shelf life.

After seven years, the deed doesn't magically disappear like a derogatory mark on your credit report. It's the forever-unseen anvil holding down the body—the dead weight. And so, I warn them that there is no blueprint, social media post, or podcast that will teach them how to disclose their entanglement with the criminal justice system. Full confession is always going to be awkward, but it plays a critical part in convincing someone that the amount of contrition equals, if not exceeds, the seriousness of the crime. The person hearing the confession wants sacrifice, be it actual or metaphorical, the guilt hanging in effigy. I let the kids know that we are the bad in the eyes of the morally good and always will be. But for all the perceived bad in me, there is equal, if not more, good that my Alabama mama instilled in me. *Seven felony convictions and now they call me "Doctor"* is the last sentence needed to win over the room.

This is the one-two punch I give them—the straight left jab followed by a haymaker to the gut—a pugilist's dream.

After my talk, Katie Owens-Murphy, who arranged my visit, tells me that she studied the kids in the room as I spoke, watching their facial expressions, mood swings, surprised looks, and most of all, curiosity, judging by the questions the young people asked after my presentation.

Katie is a professor at the University of North Alabama and coordinated my visit through the Florence-Lauderdale Public Library and Reader Riot Book Festival. She is committed to changing the narrative of incarceration; her heart is all in, and she understands the pipeline from street to prison and from juvenile to adult jail. Prison advocacy is often a thankless job, but Katie will tell you that it isn't about being thanked or admired. These kids are drowning, and no one wants to throw them a lifejacket. For a moment, Katie and I actually believe we are making a difference.

But for all the good we believe we may have done, it is not enough. Before Katie and I leave the classroom, the kids want to know when we're coming back.

We really don't know when we will come back, or if we will come back, or if anybody will come back. It's the question that hurts and haunts the most, like a kid wanting to know when the parent is coming home from the hospital when the parent really knows that it may not happen and is afraid to say so. The answers are the same: only *if* we can find a way, only *if* there is funding, only *if* the stars align three times in eight days—a whole lot of *if*s and not enough concrete answers. Outside the facility, Katie and I talk about writing grants, getting institutional support from our places of employment, and other possibilities that might allow us to come back. This is the constant struggle faced by those who work with incarcerated populations. People often say it is noble work, perhaps like being a poet, noble and important; yet people marginalize poetry every day, just like incarceration. People say they care, but where is the help, the funding, to reverse a fate all too real?

We love it, then we leave it, without much fanfare, explanation, or, sadly, change.

I will never forget the twenty young men—or the five young women seated in the back, their journey through incarceration seldom documented. Any one of these young women might have been one decision away from turning a trick to get shelter or food, but sadly, some may have had to do so. They could have been at a fork in the road, one decision away from mainline injection or skin popping, but woefully, some may have taken the road less traveled to reach that seductive needle, that false reality of comfort opioids give.

I leave, not sharing how hard it was and still is to change. If these young people are lucky enough to turn their lives around, they will soon have to make decisions like the one I made at the airport in Dallas, but that is down the road. Right now, what is most important for these individuals at the Tennessee Valley Juvenile Detention Center is that someone actually cares about their well-being, sees their humanity.

And So, It's Complicated

Question: is there clemency for the mute body screaming guilt?
I only ask because the first slap recoiled like a car backfiring, the
second became a Sunday morning sinner's wail after a long night
of bourbon, followed by another backfiring slap echoing against
the alley and gutted brownstones, then "Please don't." "Why?" is
not the question I shouted, but the woman being hit three stories
below did. Hit or slap might resonate too delicate with the ear,
more like beat; yep, he was beating the living fuck out of her.
"But I didn't do nothing," she stuttered between sobs, and "I will
go get it," and I heard it all. To peer three stories down from the
apartment in the abandoned building meant being witness to a
man beating a woman, to confront the infinite curse of addiction,
homelessness, and admit life had spiraled out of control.

The above post on Facebook describes a troubling memory of a fight
I witnessed in the mid-'90s while smoking cocaine in an abandoned
building on 14th and P Street in the Northwest section of Washington,
DC.

Without a doubt, the experience is difficult to revisit, let alone write
about, and in the post I leave it unclear as to what I did, if anything, to
prevent the assault from occurring. A poet and friend from Montgomery,
Alabama, comes across the post and emails me that same day, finding the
passage quite disturbing. She simply asks, "What did you do?" To be
honest, when I email her back, I don't completely answer the question,
because to do so would require a lengthy explanation, more than I want
to provide in an email that day.

To start, she would need to know about Debbie and the rocky relationship between the two of us. How we got sucked into the metaphorical blizzard of cocaine. Debbie and I tried to save each other from the streets, but as I've said many times before, two addicts don't make a right.

One night at the room we rented on Florida and North Capitol Street, Debbie became enraged during an argument and accused me of cheating on her with another woman. When I reminded Debbie that she sold her body to eat, get high, and pay rent, she replied that that was beside the point. We argued a bit more before I left for a few hours to avoid a physical altercation, only to return to HELL HATH NO FURY LIKE A WOMAN SCORNED scrawled in red lipstick on the mirror above the sink and all my clothes shredded with a knife and doused in human urine. This was my introduction to that saying, and I wondered what it meant in relation to her and me.

A year later I ran into her at 14th and V Street, an area that always throws me for a loop when I visit Busboys and Poets today, a restaurant, bookstore, and lounge popular in the Washington, DC, literary scene. I cannot look at Busboys and Poets for what it is; instead I see what that strip of land once represented. V Street, between 13th and 14th, was at various times an open-air market filled with women and men who sold their bodies along with those who sold what was then called crack. To understand how far Debbie and I had ventured down the rabbit hole, to give my poet friend from Alabama context about my post, and to answer her question, I would need to provide some historical perspective.

Freebase. Ready Rock. Crack.

I would explain to my poet friend that freebase is a derivative of powder cocaine, a paste that forms when the powder is cooked.

During the early '80s, young hustler chemists learned, or were taught, that this form of cocaine, once converted to freebase rock, produced quick profits. These hustler chemists then began to sell what would be called ready rock on the streets to users. This type of cocaine sold well and quickly, so the hustler chemists devised a way to increase profits by producing more rock from the freebase using a substance called comeback. The chemical ratio required a delicate balance of trial and error: greed versus good product. Because my poet friend never knew me as Hook, I would need to reveal how most of the kilos I smuggled into the United States originated from South America, wrapped in fiberglass—the cocaine so potent it created a medicinal odor that could saturate an entire room. If the product registered more than 0.9 grams on the cookup of 1.0 gram, it could be stretched with comeback to 1.25 grams for wholesale purposes or 1.5 for street soldiers who were selling directly to fiends running back and forth all night chasing a diluted high.

I would tell my poet friend that the day cocaine transitioned into ready rock isn't known, but the day crack became king in my personal realm is crystal clear.

I would tell my poet friend that customers came out of the woodwork, their frames frail, faces gaunt, pupils twinkling as if the secret to everlasting life were being sold on the low-low, an amulet of eternal possibility. Wads of cash procured from liquor store robberies, neighborhood check fraud, three-card monte games played on the bus, family theft, food stamp resale, breaking and entering, abuse of the body, and many unthinkable acts—the proceeds needed for the purchase of the beige rock that had suddenly appeared on the streets.

My poet friend would need to know that in 1989, once the first stem was lit in a back stairwell of the apartment complex in Southeast DC on Chesapeake Avenue, customers would come running back to the source of this euphoria. Not one by one, as they had in earlier times, but two by two and three by three until the fourteen-gram beige rock disappeared from my hands. It could have been a magic trick minus the *abracadabra*, but it wasn't; it could have been in a Donald Goines novel, but it wasn't.

The poet would need to be educated on how comeback created a subculture of demos known as the fake out: looks like crack, burns like crack, but smells and tastes like plastic. The most desperate of fiends would crush a peppermint until it was all white, lace it with baking soda, place it in a plastic bag or vial, and attempt to pass off the demo as authentic to someone more desperate. But the comeback, vitamin B12, yeast, or other mixing agent that added weight and yielded decent quality was a game changer. The cutting agent maximized profits, perfect in an economy where capitalism was encouraged as an American way of life. It made life easier for the addict, for the rock was precooked and offered easy access: just take it out of the plastic bag, vial, or aluminum foil and put it right into a straight shooter. So, in the mind of the young street hustler, this was an opportunity, the right environment, and a captive audience.

Along with comeback came the working fifty and later the working thirty in DC. The names are apropos, for the amounts of money they referred to were designed to fulfill two things: an addict's dream and a hustler's hope. An investment of fifty dollars could be doubled or quadrupled—or at the very least provide the opportunity to break even: smoke some, sell some, get another one, and repeat, continuing the marathon as long as you could. But the double meaning of comeback, the flip side of this fool's gold where the fiends keep coming back for more, is what's most important. There is a direct correlation between comeback and the white bloom of the '80s from the perspective of levels of chemical dependency, as if the addict were a lab rat being experimented upon. Debbie and I represented both ends of the spectrum, but we were caught in a battle we could never win.

Because my poet friend from Alabama has been to Busboys and Poets, I would ask her to imagine herself in that area in the early '90s.

Driving north on 13th Street and taking a left on V, she would have approached the spot where the establishment would appear within ten years. V was a dimly lit street rife with illicit activity: hustlers, sex workers, stick-up men. A pimp named DeAngelo ran a brothel behind the elementary school that is now Meridian Public Charter School, and in the nearby alley, a chop shop operated around the clock, taking in stolen vehicles and making them disappear more quickly than a handclap. DeAngelo left the house, and at about that time I reemerged from a homeless stint. I became a player on V Street and set up shop in the house through Pepper, a woman who had helped me survive when I became homeless on T Street years before. Pepper stayed in the back room facing the chop shop, and I fronted her and her boyfriend, Shortman, packages of powder cocaine to sell. They cooked the powder with comeback to stretch the profit.

When I ran into Debbie again, on the side of V Street that now lines a renovated park with a full-length basketball court and baseball diamond, she was trying to turn a trick to buy a working fifty from Pepper to sell to women chasing that five-minute high all night across town in Northeast DC. Because there was history between Debbie and me, and perhaps because she was jealous that Pepper was someone I trusted, Debbie asked me to watch her back before I went into the house by the alley. It was taking Debbie a long time to find a date, so she ventured closer to where Busboys and Poets is now, trying to catch a john, and we ended up one block north on 14th and W Street.

There had been love between Debbie and me, and many days I am at a loss to understand what that love was.

I would tell my poet friend about two young men, barely twenty years old, who were hanging out by the fire hydrant in the middle of the block, drinking a forty-ounce bottle of beer and counting money from drug sales. Suddenly, and without provocation, one of the men began to chastise Debbie for walking the streets, accusing her of selling demos to their clientele. Maybe his mother and sisters were in the same predicament: walking the streets, trying to feed their physical and mental hunger, but clearly, there was disdain for what Debbie represented. Debbie, not one to back down, began a verbal exchange with the guy about not selling demos; things escalated quickly, and the dude slapped her in the face while his partner remained silent in the background.

In retrospect, maybe Debbie wanted this altercation to escalate to see if I still cared in some way, to see if I would protect her.

When he proceeded to slap her again and again, uttering "bitch" and "fuck you," I felt I had to intervene. I began to exchange knuckles with the man on W Street, and right when I appeared to be getting the better of him, his partner walked up and shattered the forty-ounce bottle against my skull, sending me to the ground in a daze. Blood trickled down my face, and then it was two on one, with body blows and foot stomps until they grew tired. We were not alone on the block, but unlike on T and V Streets, I was an outlier on W Street, so no one dared to help.

Nobody fought fair or with honor anymore, so for the people standing around, watching me get stomped, the sight was nothing unusual.

As I would tell my poet friend, however, the story on W Street does not end with body blows and foot stomps. I would tell her that pride is a dangerous thing on the street. Pride will cause one to make rash decisions that may affect the future in ways unimaginable.

Pepper's boyfriend, Shortman, owned a .45. When I returned to V Street and went to their rented room, blood trickling down my face and smeared on my shirt, the .45 was the only thing on my mind—that and putting bullet holes in the two men on W. I wanted to hunt them down and feel the revenge while squeezing the trigger.

The streets create the animal, the rage, the coldheartedness toward another human being—it turns one into jagged edges, broken shards of glass.

Perhaps thinking it through in ways that I could not, Pepper and
Shortman blocked the exit to the door, preventing me from leaving after
they gave me the gun. Pepper looked me in the eye, as if to ask, *Is it worth
it?* Wisdom sometimes comes in unexpected ways.

Both Shortman and Pepper had the kind of street credibility I wanted,
but perhaps it came with ghosts that would never stop haunting them.
On more than one occasion I'd been told I didn't belong, and at this
moment I heard it again, not in words spoken but by the blocking of the
door. In the distant future I would know what it meant to try to take a
person's life, to think someone died and rejoice in that death, only to
want to take everything back the next morning, like it never happened.

Pepper and Shortman were trying to tell me what I would come to
know later.

HELL HATH NO FURY LIKE A WOMAN SCORNED. The fact that a woman
was getting beaten by a man did bother me, but the memory of body
blows and foot stomps and the forty-ounce bottle cracked against my
head with subsequent stitches and a scar—the price for trying to defend
a woman—still remained. Hope is an illusion more times than not, but
I hoped that the woman getting beaten in the alley would somehow
survive. Often memories are manipulated to present the picture we want
to believe as truth, when in actuality we lie through memory, re-creating
a series of events in our head to make a tragic event seem more palpable.
I've realized that my scorn for Debbie came from the fact that I refused
to see her as a complete human being, that I placed too much value on
perception. In her eyes she had made the ultimate sacrifice by selling her
body, and she demanded the kind of loyalty in return that I could not
give. Two years after that altercation, I ended up homeless once again,
smoking cocaine in that abandoned row house and listening to a woman
get physically assaulted in the alley. I would tell my poet friend that
memory will eat your ass alive. When I heard the lady being assaulted,
I remembered the beating I had taken, the fact that no one had come
to help. I knew that I could not intervene now because these streets can
turn violent in a heartbeat. No amount of rehabilitation can block that
memory.

Poet-in-Residence: Motivation

In 2016 I became writer-in-residence at the University of the District of Columbia, an institution unafraid to admit, and then award a bachelor's degree to, a returning citizen with seven felony convictions. The transition to college life had been arduous at best, challenging me to study very hard to master fundamental concepts I should have learned years earlier. I had not been in a classroom in more than two decades, and I spent many nights dusting off brain cells in my one-room efficiency on West Virginia Avenue near a now-revitalized H Street in Northeast DC. The main reason I returned to college was to become a poet, and, years later, I did become a poet. But more than that, I was able to have an impact, through poetry, in a city that almost ate me alive.

As part of my residency at UDC, I taught a nonfiction workshop with twelve undergraduate students twice a month, commuting on Amtrak from New York. During those trips I revisited places from my former life as a reminder of how far I'd come. I went back to the abandoned buildings I once slept in, like the gutted row house in Adams Morgan where I had lain on the floor in the below-freezing temperature, using a plastic tarp for a blanket. I sought out places where I had tried to take someone's life, such as the parking spot on 13th and Euclid where I had blasted multiple hollow-point bullets through the windshield of a van, or where I had almost lost my own life, in the Clifton Terrace projects about three blocks away, after a drug deal gone bad.

I remember the location of every rooming house I was evicted from—the first one at 9th and French, then 13th and T, 14th and R, 1st and O, 5th and N—so I went back to each spot, reliving moments when I existed somewhere between the living and the could-be-dead. Those neighborhoods have been gentrified, the places I left behind all but erased. Now I do exist among the living.

In 2018 I served as the first poet-in-residence at the Civil Rights Corps in Washington, DC, a nonprofit organization dedicated to challenging systemic injustice in the United States. The idea that poetry could have a meaningful impact on criminal justice might seem far-fetched, but the CRC is willing to use unconventional methods to shed light on unjust practices. The poems are available on the CRC's website; they are also displayed on the walls of its office in Northwest DC, not far from MCI Telecommunications, where I worked in the mid-'80s before quitting to embark on an eighteen-year cocaine odyssey.

The eager young lawyers at the CRC, led by founder and executive director Alec Karakatsanis, invited me to collaborate with them to search for ways that literature could make an impact, providing an opportunity for me to use my past for a greater good. My first task was to address the unfairness of the American bail system and the unreasonable require-ments for probation. The idea was to use poetry to help educate the public on the illegal ways in which people are detained, to reveal the harshness of a system that is cruel to those who never showed cruelty.

The probation case at the CRC that caught my attention more than any other involved Karen McNeil of Giles County, Tennessee. On the surface, Karen and I had very little in common. She is white and I am Black. Although we both grew up in the South, she in Tennessee and I in Alabama, we conceivably had very different childhoods. Yet her story struck a chord.

Karen had been arrested in 2015 for driving on a revoked license. She was initially put on four months' probation and ordered to pay $426 in fines and fees, $45 a month to the for-profit company contracted by the county to supervise her, and $45 for each random drug test she was required to take, even though her offense had nothing to do with drugs.

Karen's respiratory issues required her to use an oxygen tank, and she lived on disability and food stamps. Because she did not want to go to jail, she decided to pay the probation fees rather than continue to pay rent, so she moved into a tent. She still couldn't keep up with the payments, so she was arrested again and sentenced to more probation, lengthening the misery—and ensuring that the private company would continue collecting fees. What hit hardest for me was that although her probation stretched to two years, with her fees more than double the initial fine, Karen landed in jail anyway after missing a probation appear-ance because she was in the hospital.

Like I said, on the surface we appeared to be different, but I, too, knew what it was like to sleep under an assemblage of stars, not knowing when a bath would be possible. I, too, had violated probation more than once, and each time, money was the issue. This is the love the criminal justice system gives, as in, no love at all.

Karen's troubles were not in vain. Giles County ultimately agreed to cease using private probation companies after the CRC filed a $2 million class-action lawsuit, with Karen named as one of the plaintiffs.

No entity within the massive wheel sheds a tear or cries because of a person's dire circumstances. They mean nothing in the eyes of justice. What sealed our fate as soul mates was this passage in the CRC's brief: "During a probation meeting after losing her home, Ms. McNeil told her probation officer that she was sleeping by the creek. The officer demanded money anyway." I, too, have experienced that lack of sympathy: during a hearing on whether my prison sentence could be modified, a prosecutor told the judge that I would never amount to anything regardless of how hard I tried and that I should be sent back to prison.

Six months into my residency at the CRC, I visited a class at the Borough of Manhattan Community College, part of the City University of New York, to talk about the writing life.

During my visit, we also talked about my investment in social advocacy and prison reform. After reading an excerpt from my essay-in-progress about prison and the stereotypes that come from being associated with prison, the students and I engaged in a conversation that stayed with me long afterward. The discussion began after a woman from Ghana asked a series of questions: What was and is your motivation? How were you able to stay focused after prison, and what drives you every day to not go back to the place you left? I confessed to her and to the class that my motivation stemmed from the pain and suffering I caused those closest to me. While on the streets, the people I hung with, and wreaked havoc with, swore that we were a family unit, and I believed this declaration until the day I entered prison, never to see them again.

I marveled at weekend visits in state prison. The housing unit would be filled with canary chatter and excitement, as those expecting visitors changed into street clothes sent from loved ones. Many wore their hair in perfect cornrows created by the designated hair braider in the unit. Some sported Afros, Philly Fades, or tapers, saturating themselves in baby powder and lotion to smell good, waiting to hear their surnames called so that the prized visit could begin.

But since I can't re-create something I've never experienced, I don't know how to get from the housing unit to the visiting room at Roxbury—the corridors you have to walk down, the markers where the guards search you in plastic gloves from head to toe and then up the crack of your ass. I don't know the seating arrangements, nor have I ever seen the pure joy in a person's eyes the moment the visit begins. I can't tell you the setup of the vending machines, or the type of snacks one could purchase while in the visiting room.

I don't know and can't tell you, because I never received a visit at Roxbury.

My real family—the mother who birthed me prematurely, the father who raised me to not go to jail, and the sister who never said no to her big brother—made the real sacrifices only unconditional love can justify. This family did not hang up the phone when the prerecorded operator recited, "You have a collect call from inmate 289-128, Randall Horton, at Roxbury Correctional Institution." Instead, my family accepted the call, allowing us to talk for fifteen minutes. Each phone call cost thirty dollars, and if we talked twice a week, the monthly phone bill would amount to two hundred forty dollars. This sum was in addition to the cost of necessary items from commissary, like real soap or toothpaste that didn't have your breath smelling bad after five minutes, deodorant that actually kept you smelling decent, and snacks to satisfy the hunger that set in after evening lock-in. Although I would have loved a visit, the cost of airfare and lodging would have been astronomical, so phone calls made the most sense, even if the bills made us feel robbed.

The woman from Ghana seemed adamant in wanting to know what motivated me, and to answer this complicated question, I tried to provide as much context as possible.

I plowed deep into one of my memories as I spoke to the class. The street arteries—those pockmarked veins where the homeless congregate—are brutal. To survive the seasons while destitute and adrift, you need extensive knowledge of places to obtain food, the intricate details of shelters—times of entry and departure, who gives the free train passes—and where to shower, piss, take a crap. The abandoned buildings where one could burn the stem or stab a vein while risking the pistol or the blade are all too real—as in, tangible fragments of the insane.

Drug addiction is a cycle—of struggling to stay clean and ultimately relapsing, only to repeat, reset, and flail back further into the dark abyss of the insane. The lack of lodging to shield from the elements creates a deadly lover: as it medicates, tempts, becomes foe rather than ally, it is also an inner voice seductively calling and begging for company. It is misery disguised as euphoria. At one time, I told the woman from Ghana, this is how I lived. But, of course, she and the class would need more context in terms of my journey.

Labor pools—businesses advertising daily work, daily pay—were popular with the homeless community in Washington, DC, during the '80s.

These establishments preyed on the economically deprived, the addicted, and the mentally challenged. To say it was a setup, a trick bag, a trap, a conspiracy to further keep down those denied the American dream, is not a leap into the fantastical. I asked the Ghanaian woman to consider the evidence: at 4:30 A.M., shelter workers tap the army cot with a nightstick, and by 5:00 A.M., that homeless body needs to be a memory. At 5:30 A.M., many of those warm bodies crowd the labor pools hoping to catch a job ticket. The rules are that the first to come will be the first to obtain backbreaking work: digging ditches with a shovel, demolition work with a sledgehammer, mixing mortar with a stick on a twenty-foot scaffold, hot-tar roofing with a mop on plywood— job descriptions synonymous with dirt and grime, and, yes, women are welcome to join the exploited. After eight hours or more of hard labor, often one rung above migrant-worker conditions, for minimum wage, the workers head back to the labor pool for a $32 check after taxes.

One block from the labor pool, the liquor store charges $3.50 to cash the check without government identification. Both entities are in cahoots for the bottom line—money.

Inside the store, a thirty-two-ounce bottle of malt liquor is available for $2. On the street, crack (cocaine powder cooked up and stretched with vitamin B12, procaine, or comeback to maximize profits) is obtainable in red and green caps bought in New York City for $5 and resold in DC for $10 each or two for $18. The year is 1992 and a gentrified landscape is still on the horizon for the Shaw neighborhood of Washington, DC, so one has a choice of which abandoned building to get high in. The crack stem, a twisted-off car antenna wrapped in electric tape, sizzles with the flick of a lighter in this mildewed structure, white smoke funneling so thick you could cut it with a knife. The high is a temporary and temporal escape from the battered condition of the body, but the journey always boomerangs back to the real. Once the last chipped pebble is gone, the brain relays a million signals, some deadly.

It tries to suppress this urge, but often the mind fails its own morality, and the craving for *more* wins with an act of crime.

I inform the Ghanaian woman along with the class that homelessness is a difficult cycle to break, a revolving door that never stops, never allows you to get a foothold in society. Days blend into an infinity of time, and the external world is inconsequential. People look through your body as if it were invisible, erased—they assume, therefore do not speak, only turn their heads—but the silence is deafening. You become the tragic figure capable of revolting against humanity. Insurrection often leads to incarceration and recidivism because the "desperate" are not bound by moral conviction, and survival does not regard personal feelings or human dignity.

Survival only cares about how to avoid sleepwalking while inside a maze of false turns.

I was trapped in this maze for extended periods in Washington, DC— the nomadic existence of the unseen. While homeless, I worked day labor or stole during the light and got high and stole again in the dark. When I didn't sleep in the shelters, I slept in my Suzuki Samurai, most of the time never venturing beyond a ten-block radius of 13th and T Street. The Samurai was a reminder, a status symbol for drug dealers, showing that I was one of those capable of capitalizing, could play the game and prosper. It was my only possession that created the illusion that I was not homeless, though I was. By day, I drove the car to get to jobs that demanded hard work—by night, I parked and roamed the streets with my fellow cohorts.

Describing the only break from this daze begins with a historical review of 9th and N Street, one year before a friend would be shot in the head seven times with a .357 pistol.

Because I am guessing the woman from Ghana had not been in the United States for long, I gave her a clear description of what it was like to live in Washington, DC, during the '80s. I let her know that in 1983 the interactions on 9th and N had already been established, long before I moved there. It was the epitome of what would be tagged as a red-light district. Sex workers provided the setting in this neighborhood, present-ing illusion as fantasy, as tangible flesh. No actual red lights beaconed, but their hue was everywhere. Red, the color of bloodshot eyes. Red, the color of burned thumbs cooling base pipes. Red, staining the inside of a used syringe littering the street. Red wigs. Red leg warmers. Red bikinis with a thong strap running up the crack of somebody's child's ass. But most of all, that invisible red, the red of danger, of what lurks and waits, the unseen, was the electric current that kept the block lit.

Between the stop-and-go traffic of men cheating on their wives and lovers there were day laborers searching for intimacy who lacked the time or means for romance alongside other men offering drugs in exchange for sex. There was a certain etiquette in that no faction intruded on the other's territorial space to make money, mainline, or burn a glass bowl stuffed with Chore Boy and freebase. Crack would not appear as a commodified street product for another five years; in the meantime, users bought powder cocaine and cooked it up with baking soda into freebase. Metal stems fashioned from car antennas would replace glass bowls and butane torches, providing easy access to a high that, once achieved, proved hard to forget.

Here I straddled life as a college student and a drug dealer.

I joined this soon-to-be-extended narrative in medias res, my first indoctrination to that other DC, the one that didn't recover from the riots of the '60s, where addiction commanded you to sell your soul and your dignity, forcing you into an endless labyrinth with no exit.

My first overdose scare came in the apartment at 9th and N, after cooking up a new package of Peruvian flake from Miami and reducing it to oil so that it could harden and be burned.

After the initial thrust of white smoke funneled through the Pyrex bowl into my lungs, the rush I felt turned into uncontrollable hoofbeats in my chest, my heart beating harder than a moth's wings next to a light bulb; the air, the precious oxygen that gave me strength to move, became nonexistent, and I gasped repeatedly, trying to breathe. Unable to calibrate my body parts to function as one entity, I wandered outside into a blizzard, half a foot of snow already on the ground. My roommate's screams snapped me back to consciousness, along with the ice forming on my feet. This was a reality the woman from Ghana could not comprehend, but she and the rest of the class listened intently, trying to absorb as much information as they could.

I decided to fast-forward my reflection-in-progress to 1990, a year after I was forced to stay away from Eleuthera, the island in the Bahamas where I had been smuggling cocaine into the United States.

I told the class that my drug empire came tumbling down because of jealous business partners who tried to set up a deal without my knowledge and ended up getting arrested while coming through US Customs in Miami with cocaine strapped to their bodies. No one could be sure that my former business partners did not snitch me out, so I agreed to stay away from Eleuthera for a while. I expected my exile to last only a few months, but instead it lasted several years. After struggling to stay financially afloat, I became a homeless yet functioning addict, able to disguise my physical and emotional state.

I knew how to take advantage of free services to preserve the illusion of normalcy, when inside I was a fragmented train wreck.

While staying at a homeless shelter on 14th and R Street, I called my sister one night and learned that I needed to be in Birmingham in two weeks for her wedding. She wanted me to be a part of the ceremony, though at the time I had no money or prospects of money, only the day-labor routine that was pushing me further into addiction. Consequently, I made myself a promise to save money by not getting high, by eating the free food provided in the evenings by So Others Might Eat (SOME) and the Martha's Table food wagon, and by meeting shelter deadlines so that I could get eight hours of sleep a night and be ready for the 4:30 A.M. tap on the army cot to wake up and report for work. I could not miss my sister's wedding.

Though simple, the task was monumental since at this point in my life, temptation and I were conjoined twins.

One day, I sat in my Samurai, parked directly across from my old apartment at 9th and N, agonizing over the promise I had made to myself a week earlier. More than two hundred and fifty dollars lined my pockets, the result of ten-hour days at regular pay, two nights of operating my car as a gypsy cab at the Greyhound bus station, and not getting high. I should not have veered from the already charted path for that day—to cash my check and head straight for the shelter on Rhode Island Avenue to sleep, wake up at the usual time, and take I-66 to Birmingham—but I did.

Instead, I ended up taking the man who worked with me to cop a working fifty. I allowed him to test the product in my car, where I could hear the sizzle of crack and imagine the smoke numbing my body. I emphasized to the woman from Ghana, who I am quite sure had no point of reference in terms of smoking cocaine, that it's the memory that eats at you, the forget-me-nots invoked by the sound, the smoke, and the medicinal smell. The money in your pocket is a gateway to that feel-good memory, a feeling to die for.

Stopping at 1st and Bates Street to pick up two women willing to sacrifice their bodies as collateral for a hit was probably not a good idea, either. If objectification is a delicate balance, all three of us were willing participants ruled by a power greater than ourselves. One of the women offered a pull from her crack-caked glass stem in a "tourist home," a fancy name for whorehouse. Like the biblical Adam, I acquiesced to my own weakness, grabbed the stem, and the race began: back and forth to the dope man until the two women left me in the car for good, taking my last twenty dollars to cop a rock I never saw. In my possession at the time of their departure: a full tank of gas, a bottle of Wild Irish Rose, and guilt eating a hole in my stomach. The burnt-orange glow from hot boxing a Newport kept me preoccupied until all that was left was the butt, and me.

Dead weight makes one wonder how to kill the self for the sake of self—a self lost.

I could not fathom or dream of a suicide scenario, though, so I cranked the Samurai, drove south on 9th Street, hit a right on Constitution Avenue, and let the radiance from cherry blossoms in bloom along with the streetlights lead the way to I-66. The thing with addiction and lying is that the addicted actually believe the lie to the point of rigorous and irrational defense of said lie. *How* I would make it to Birmingham with no money didn't matter, it was the *will* to make it there, pushed over the edge of the rational to the irrational, that was paramount. By the time the Samurai reached I-81 South, the medicating substances had lost their power, night had turned into day, and I began pounding on the steering wheel, asking, *What the fuck is the matter with you, Randall?*

The gas needle gradually moved from full to a quarter tank. I hopped off the interstate three times before spotting a gas station still willing to trust people.

PUMP FIRST, PAY INSIDE, the sign read. Video surveillance would show that a Black man pulled to the outside lane of the third island in his Samurai—which had Alabama tags, so no front license plate—used pump 16, filled up with super supreme unleaded, replaced the pump, twisted the gas cap back on, opened the car door as if to retrieve a credit card but instead slid into the seat, closed the door, lodged the Samurai in drive, pulled out slowly as though he owned the damn place, made a left onto the two-lane street, eased over to the right, then went down the curved ramp heading south on the interstate. In all of the wedding photos in which I appear, no one would know this narrative, the glances in the rearview, the anxiety, the shortness of breath, let alone 9th Street and what had happened there. The photos are a misrepresentation of an image, an elusive doubling of myself, hiding the worst of the twelve-hour odyssey from DC to Birmingham while projecting a semblance of normalcy and self-confidence. My sister didn't know how I stole gas four times, the last time just outside of Huntsville, Alabama, to get home.

I could never have lived with myself had I not shown up for the wedding, and I feel the same way today—I never want to disappoint my sister, because she believes in me.

After providing this lengthy but much-needed context for the answer to the woman from Ghana's first question, I told the class about the case of Karen McNeil from Tennessee. I wanted the students to see that although Karen and I had lived different lives, I still empathized with her and understood the despair she felt. At that point I read aloud an email I received from Lily Bou of the Civil Rights Corps:

Dear Randall,

I work as an investigator at Civil Rights Corps, and I had the chance to hear you read some of your poetry at CRC's event at the Riverside Church in Harlem a few months ago. I was particularly moved by your poem about Karen McNeil. I have gotten to know Karen a bit over the course of my visits to Giles County. She is a truly special and extremely resilient woman, and I loved how you memorialized her story in your work.

I wanted to let you know that I read your poem to Karen when I was last in Giles. She was deeply touched by the poem—and by the fact that the story of what happened to her, what this probation scheme had done to her, was being shared widely. She couldn't believe that her story was being shared in New York City, of all places! It was an incredibly powerful moment, and Karen was moved to tears.

This is just a note to thank you for the poem, and for your work generally. There is so much power in sharing these stories, particularly through art, and I know Karen appreciated the way you honored her in your writing.

All the best,

Lily

I informed the class that it was only after being in prison, and then getting the opportunity to have the semblance of a life, that I began to think about the good I could achieve in this world.

I don't need or want a pat on the back for doing what human beings should be doing, and that is helping each other.

I told the students that I am motivated by the people I meet in juvenile detention centers across the country, such as the young men and women who attended a poetry workshop I did at Pima County Juvenile Detention Center in Tucson, Arizona. Before the workshop began, I showed a video clip of me reading an excerpt from my memoir, *Hook*, mainly for the lyrical qualities of the piece, with its themes of gunplay and violence that end in regret. On this particular day, after the clip played, one of the young men seated among the gray metal tables along the front anointed me an OG (original gangster). The marvel in his grin was matched by the sparkle in his eye and the smugness with which he made his declaration. Then he began an interrogation, wanting to know all the intricate experiences every other young man in the room wanted to know regarding the life of a dealer: the money, the cars, the high life. This was disheartening, but a reality I have come to accept and expect.

My answers skipped over the glorification and dwelled on the many lonely nights—the night screams, the night terror, the isolation, the uncomfortable conversations about prison rape.

Then the young men in the room asked how I came to be a writer, an occupation they seemed to respect, especially when the writer could speak their language. I brought up the group I was a part of in county jail and the assignments we were given to write about the suffering we had caused others. By reliving my narrative from various points of view, I was better able to analyze and restructure my life's purpose. Over time, the power of the imagination—thinking creatively and drawing on memory at times—allowed me to come to grips with my past. By the time I recounted every harsh reality I endured as a result of being an OG, the whole room concurred that it wasn't worth it.

My narrative complete, the entire class at the Borough of Manhattan Community College proceeded to clap, cheer, and pump their fists, and I was relieved that I never lost them during my lengthy explanation, which took them down many avenues.

Maybe I will never be able to fully answer the young woman from Ghana's question about what motivates me; but each time I try, I seem to get a little bit closer to discovering that elusive truth. It is a question I am asked a lot, and I think in some way, we as human beings are always looking for some kind of blueprint. Even though I took the class on a narrative journey, delving into the personal to make correlations and a larger point, I ultimately taught them one simple lesson, and that was to show up every day, and when it seems all is lost, to not give up, because like an addict that relapses, giving up makes the problem ten times worse. Showing up every day offered me a pathway to being a writer, giving me the opportunity to overcome obstacles standing in the way of progress. Before I left I told the class that if they ever encountered a Karen McNeil in the world, they should offer help, compassion, empathy, and grace. They said they would, and I'm thinking that maybe hope isn't an illusion after all.

PART 3

1303 T Street: Collateral Damage

Shady Grove Metro station marks the beginning or the end of the red line in Washington, DC, depending on where one embarks.

PLAY ALL DAY, advertised in red, appears on a rectangular placard tacked to the car's wall. Each person riding the train meditates in the wake of an invisible drone, trying to assimilate into what it means to be American—from clothes to makeup wreaking of made-up. Here is the well-kept secret: no one in the train car is aware of the passenger who transitioned from convict to teacher—the now writer-in-residence at the University of the District of Columbia who commutes from Harlem once a week to teach the art of memoir—the poet formerly known as Hook. To be honest, it's all a sham, this constant identification—to be continually placed in a box of expectations and past transgressions. True, a different theme of apprehension would write itself out if the people on the train knew the chronicles of the once-forgotten like me.

To be sure, it's a different District of Columbia these days, and I no longer belong here. Chocolate City has become Twirl City, at best. The attractions of this used-to-be oasis of Blackness in the early '80s have dissipated, some for the good, a lot for the bad. There is an aesthetic missing, but memory can be nostalgic to a fault. Maybe I want to remember hell and misfortune as the good-time ride, or that the tragedy I endured actually masqueraded as divine comedy hidden in adventure.

Memory also has a way of fading, minus the gunshots, the blade stabs, and the deaths that could have been if the fired bullets had reached their intended target.

To reach my final destination on the train, I need to transfer at Gallery Place. I exit the red and board the green, once widely known among Black folk as the "nigga line" because it took forever to be built in this ever-changing city. The breaking of dirt ensued after the first dog walkers and pooper scoopers with mortgages, 401(k)s, and disposable income began to brave the transition from hood to haven, much like the original criminals who arrived on the *Mayflower* to build a new world rooted in erasure. I exit the train at U Street/African-American Civil War Memorial/Cardozo station like a magnet pulled to memory, because revisiting collateral damage of the past allows me to move toward the future I've tried to conceive. Everything has changed.

On U Street there are no sex workers flagging down cars, no teenage boys hanging on the corner with sacks full of weed or ready rock, no starry-eyed addicts searching for an escape from reality. Before I make it to 14th to hang a left, then another left down T Street (because I want to take the long route), I can't help but notice the twenty-four-hour Rite Aid and the rooftop taverns juxtaposed against luxury apartments. These businesses have replaced the abandoned warehouse that once stretched a block, where those sex workers flagging down cars escorted their tricks to treat them to a fool's dream.

This is the same block where I got high in a vacated structure reeking of feces and urine and strewn with dirty needles, used condoms, and empty liquor bottles.

It is here where I day-labored for a homeless bricklayer named Rock Steady, who brought me on to help build the foundation for a new building in place of a warehouse that had been demolished. I poured mortar into a five-gallon bucket, hoisting it on a rope for the mud gliders to use in building the cinderblock foundation. After a week of lifting blocks and buckets, working from can't to can't in hundred-degree weather during the month of July, I quit on a Friday morning. I emphasized to the construction supervisor, "Damn the two-week wait! I need my ducats, not right now, but *rit-nah.*" Oh, yeah, I acted a natural fool until the man gave me all the money I had earned. Funny to think how Rock Steady and I labored to displace those who had squatted here, including ourselves.

The abandoned storefront where Sugar and Edwina would perform fellatio in the back alley, then search for the one-punch knockout artist Bombshell to cop a packet of Bo Jackson so all three could oil up, nod, and droop to the ground like puppets manipulated by an unseen string puller is gone—supplanted by a Starbucks coffee shop. Yum's Carry Out around the corner on 14th is another casualty. The affordable two-piece chicken with fried rice and mumbo sauce, well suited to the homeless community, did not survive gentrification. Yum's has been replaced by a high-end denim retailer that accepts used jeans for recycling as community housing insulation. Even the liquor store on the corner that once held AA/NA meetings every hour on the hour is gone.

Can't forget the 1425 building on the other side of T Street, where an old guy named Cuban operated a crack den for women only—less chance of getting robbed that way.

The women needed to buy there, smoke there, and tweak there before running out the door to flag a bevy of cars to repeat the process. One woman, named Taboo, tried to pickpocket a john there and got lighter fluid poured on her face. When the john lit Taboo up, she morphed into a glowing matchstick as she ran down T Street at midnight. To walk down T Street now means to enter another landscape, one much different from what I recall. There is now a big plaque that reads, CITY WITHIN A CITY/GREATER U STREET HERITAGE TRAIL: *A MAGIC PLACE*, and photos of Louis Armstrong and Sarah Vaughan from the 1940s are posted on the former site of Club Bali, a prominent nightspot in one of the few integrated social scenes in the city. The block is no longer the block it once was. The crumbling concrete sidewalks are now paved with red brick. After the death of Mr. Woody, a former Metro worker who owned a house at 1324, his family sold low to the swirling vultures. The house has since been converted into two apartments.

Mrs. Trudy and Joe Gregory and their six kids never owned the house they resided in at 1326, but they lived on T Street for eighteen years before moving to Clifton Terrace apartments when the rent got too high. On the other side of the street, at 1345, Tally R. Holmes's Attorney-at-Law office remains, though he has long since passed away. Tally earned a law degree from Howard University back in the '60s, owned several rental apartments on the block, and provided maintenance jobs to the homeless and addicted. The people living at 1325 will never know that their row house was a common meeting place for the homeless to drink liquor and smoke cocaine; if only their basement stairwell could talk. And then, there it is, the "it" being the house, the house being 1303, sporting a fresh coat of blue paint on the brick facade and crisp white on the trim and front-porch columns. White wooden blinds appear in the first-floor windows for privacy. The front yard, landscaped with shrubbery and decorative mulch, has a sign planted in the dirt that read PROTECTED BY ULTRA GUARD SECURITY SYSTEMS.

This house was once synonymous with death.

It happened like this: on the other side of midnight, at about three in the morning—based on a reliable tip from a woman playing both ends to the middle—William D. Baker, Eric T. Franklin, Jamal R. Sampson, and Bryant C. Woodland went to the back of 1303 and initiated a *bash* with the sole of a Timberland boot through the kitchen door, armed with enough firepower to subtract a muthafucka from the living. The goal was to jack ten kilos of powder and one hundred thousand dollars from Gary Lyles, a dealer, I-95 smuggler, and my longtime friend who rented a room on the first floor near the front entrance.

The owner of the house, John Glenn, slept upstairs in the same room he grew up in, while his childhood friend, the one-punch knockout artist Bombshell, was allowed to sleep on the bedroom floor after a night of getting high and watching reruns on television. Both individuals escaped through the window and leapt onto the ground from the second-floor roof, their landing cushioned by twelve inches of snow. David Buford, a play brother to John, rented the upstairs room near the stair landing; he was bludgeoned with a machete. At the flash point of the break-in, Donald Pinkney was smoking a blunt and preoccupied with a Play-Station game; he was shot and killed on bended knees, begging for his life. The target of the operation, Gary, fled unharmed, only because he responded in kind to the rapid succession of gunfire, leaving a silent house of documented horror.

At noon, before lock-in at Seven Locks on August 5, 1999, this event was breaking news on the local ABC affiliate.

I witnessed the news flash in a county-issued blue jumper and flip-flops, watching television in the day room of my dorm unit. That could have been me chilling with the blunt next to Pinkney, one of those fired bullets having the name RANDALL on it. I had once slept in the same room David occupied, crashed on the same floor Bombshell had, drank and smoked in the room where Gary would need to crouch behind a yellow antique dresser in a gun battle for his life. The house at 1303 T Street held a special place in my heart, and so I feel partly responsible for Pinkney's death. Not only that, these events caused my friend John to lose his house, the one his dad bought in 1928 for $15,000 (equal to about $226,000 today), which, through gentrification, is now worth more than $1 million.

My relationship to 1303 began during my once-homeless state.

I repeatedly watched people slide keys into the door lock, then open and close the door—something so simple that it seemed like make-believe, yet happened only in other people's lives, not mine. After the shelters, abandoned buildings, and cars I lived in, along with a furnished rented room, which I was kicked out of for nonpayment after a night of cocaine binging, John gave me the opportunity to turn "make-believe" into reality. Getting off the bus at 14th Street to head home, John could never avoid walking by the house on T Street whose location we homeless guys referred to as "under the tree."

"Under the tree" was in the yard of the abandoned row house at 1325, a place where Andy, Joe, Lilton, Dwayne, Rock Steady, Bombshell, Tonio, and I congregated during the day to drink thirty-two ounces of cheap beer and pints of rotgut vodka and to plot our next move—how to make money appear in our pockets, by hook or by crook, so that we could smoke cocaine and medicate misery presented as reality. These were the goals for the under-the-tree crew. John would stop, drink, talk to the guys under the tree as if he were one of them, except that he wasn't and had a place to call home. John eventually invited me down to his house on the corner, where we would smoke in his upstairs room, talk about sports, his part-time classes at UDC, my time at Howard, and how we both wanted to further our education.

I considered John kindred not only because of his academic aspirations, but also because our discourse went beyond the superficial street stuff. He vaguely knew of me from my dealings with the woman named Jo-Jo who grew up across the street, daughter to Mrs. Trudy and Joe, a woman who crossed US Customs in Miami with cocaine strapped down the inside of her thighs, in the crack of her ass, the middle of her back, and any other part of the body that could avoid detection. John had tried some of that Bahama coke from Jo-Jo and knew me as this big-time smuggler, but no one cares about that when you are wallowing at the bottom.

The fall is always a blue note in four-four time, and when I fell, I fell right onto T Street.

When John invited me to live in his house, we needed to clear the arrangement with his ninety-year-old dad and eighty-eight-year-old aunt Celie, who both lived there. Shortly after the green light that gave me stable housing and an address to put on a job application, I secured employment as a temporary mail clerk on 5th Street and Rhode Island

Avenue. Staying with John allowed me to adopt Celie as a moral compass. When Celie and I had conversations in her room (Celie was
bedridden), she gave me encouragement, talked to me with affirmation
and love, and made me feel human, like maybe I mattered in the grand
scheme of the human condition. I came to love this woman like family.

Celie often held my weekly paycheck for me so that it would not
evaporate in one night. To ask for money, I needed to look into the
eighty-eight-year-old woman's eyes and be judged for the fiend I had
become. I knew this, and didn't want that—so I never asked late at
night, when that jones called for a refill of that feel-good. What is more
crucial to this story, however, is the simultaneous reemergence of my
longtime drug connections Craig Davis and Gary Lyles. These two men
are the lynchpin.

One day, while John and I were sitting on the front steps of 1303,
Craig pulled up in a Lexus and shouted, "Hook, we back on! Time to
get your shit together!"

John wanted to know who this dude was, reclining in the driver's
seat and wearing shades darker than black ice. I hadn't seen Craig since
he entered federal prison for a charge of conspiracy to sell two kilos of
powder in Prince Georges County. When I walked up to the car, I knew
Craig would ask why I was on T Street damn near homeless. Instead, he
told me, "Hook, everything back on. We gonna buy this house uptown
on Whittier. My old man, Bobby, put me on location with ten kilos. We
gonna handle this thing right this time. Boy, you done hit the lottery."
By now he was smiling and nodding, as though keeping time to a Curtis
Mayfield soundtrack in his head: "I'm your mama, I'm your daddy / I'm
that nigga in the alley." Craig proceeded to inform me that his father,
Bobby, was supplying cocaine to a kingpin whom our friend Gary was
connected to in Northeast DC. The kingpin bought fifty to one hundred
kilos a month, easy. Craig was getting access to five to ten from his dad.
In other words, Craig was going to rescue me from T. This is how I
reconnected with Gary after years of not seeing him.

So, all that to say, John met Gary through me, and when I moved
uptown, Gary left his mother's row house on South Dakota Avenue and
moved in to the front room of 1303.

Soon after Gary moved in, John's father died and Aunt Celie had
to be placed in a convalescent home. Within two years, 1303 became
a stash house and operating point for Gary. Because he would often

conduct deals for his supplier at the house, on any given night there could be close to a million dollars dripping through the money machine. Gary would break down kilos of powder into smaller weights on a triple-beam balance or digital scale while conducting transactions with clients he had known for ten years. All this occurred with John and David living in the house. Those two would come to feel the law of unintended consequences.

After I moved out, I continued to stop by and sit in that front room, doing deals with Gary, who had no problem with possessing a firearm despite his felony convictions. Often, after transacting some kind of deal, we sat and occasionally got high while reflecting on how everything was going smoothly. Gary would smoke ready rock in a makeshift ash bowl while I rolled tobacco with crushed ready rock and smoked it like a joint. We both possessed an affinity for aged cognac, or brandy when the cash flow wasn't as great. Every once in a while, Gary pulled out his .380 pistol, cleaned it, oiled the barrel, and loaded the ammunition.

Gary would always offer, "You never know, Hook. Always got to be ready for something to pop off," the gun's silver shine bouncing off the gold crown in his mouth.

I rode shotgun with Gary the day he came in possession of the .380, which he received courtesy of a deal gone bad in the Bottom, or, if you prefer its proper name, Miami. The middleman to the purchaser and the supplier was a mechanic who owned an auto shop and specialized in moving gas tanks to make room for kilos of powder to be transported north on I-95. The mechanic got swindled out of the eighteen thousand dollars that Gary had given him to cop the drugs, and instead of inserting a bullet in the mechanic's brain, Gary's supplier decided to let it go, figuring the risk wasn't worth the reward. The .380 was presented as a thank-you from the mechanic. I originally made the trip in hopes of catching a twin engine to Eleuthera, in the Bahamas, where I would meet my connection and negotiate a cocaine shipment to be brought over on a plane or boat. That plan was pushed back when we took the loss.

David would testify at trial that he was in his second-floor bedroom—the same bedroom where I sat at night talking with Aunt Celie—when he heard *pop-pop-pop-pop-pop-pop*.

This strange but known succession of sounds prompted David to run down the hall to John's room in a moment of panic; out of the corner of his eye, David noticed a person coming up the stairs, and he doubled back into a six-foot slender man at the landing with dark clothing and ski mask moving directly toward him with a .45 and a machete.

Running back into the .45, David heard the command, "Spread eagle, on the floor," but reached for the assailant's gun and knocked it down. While the .45 barreled down the stairs, metal ricocheting against wood, the assailant, later identified as Jamal R. Sampson, used his machete and went to work on David, who would later be hospitalized for five days, forty staples in his left arm and thirty-five to forty staples in his gut, not to mention three stab wounds in the head. One of the paramedics testified that the sheer volume of blood on the floor caused him to slip and slide.

With the jack in progress and David being gutted like a bluegill upstairs, Gary faced his *You never know, Hook* moment of truth.

Gary testified that he initially jumped out of bed after the *bash* and the *pop-pop-pop-pop-pop-pop*. He dropped to the floor, crouched behind the yellow antique dresser, and steadied his gun. One of the assailants, William D. Baker, made his way to the front room, stuck his arm and then head around Gary's door, and began firing randomly. Gary, understanding that the moment of truth was upon him, and that a scared man can't live, fired his .380, hitting Baker in the neck. Baker went reeling back down the hallway critically injured, yelling, "I'm hit, Jamal, I'm hit!" Meanwhile, as Gary got ready to dash out the front door, he glanced down the darkened hallway and saw a young man, likely Pinkney, lying on the floor.

I never wanted to sell to Pinkney, but I did a few times to get back on my feet after I hooked up with Craig. Pinkney understood that the quality of drugs he copped from me was unlike anything he had access to in DC—not that there weren't other avenues, but he didn't know them. Perhaps Pinkney saw my rise as a modern urban fairy tale, damn near mythical: homeless guy hooked on coke flips the script and now supplies the supplier.

Though I could have been Pinkney's supplier, I chose not to be. There were too many risks in selling small packages on the street. I was worried about getting caught by the feds, so I avoided temptations that would take me down that road.

Gary, however, began to deal with Pinkney after moving in with John. They became close, and Pinkney started spending a lot of time at 1303. Call it intuition, or reading the tea leaves, but selling large amounts of crack signaled a YIELD sign in my head; so did dealing with cats on T Street with stakes this high. Having stayed on T, both outdoors and indoors, I not only witnessed but participated in the stickups, robberies, con games, the getting over at every chance possible. I ran with cold-blooded killers whose reputations were earned fair and square, saw sex workers set up tricks who wanted illusion presented as fantasy. I knew drug dealers who had been shot as they lurked in crevices between store-fronts—in the chest, the legs, the testicles.

All this knowledge told me not to engage with Pinkney, or anybody else on T Street that sold ready rock.

A District of Columbia medical examiner concluded that Pinkney's wounds were consistent with his being on his knees at the time of the shooting, and that he died from gunshot wounds inflicted by a .45 caliber handgun—three *pop-pop-pop*s in the back, one *pop* in the front as he tried to turn around, one *pop* in the side as he dropped to his knees to beg for his life, and one *pop* in the right arm, which he tried unsuccessfully to use as a shield against the onslaught of bullets.

Pinkney would not have expired facedown in a pool of blood, excre-ment running down his pants, if I had never shown up on T Street.

My first night on T Street was spent sleeping in an abandoned car in the alley behind Jo-Jo's house. It was there that I began to learn the ways of the homeless, using T street as an operating base to survive. I was originally an outlier, a person who looked like he didn't belong, who followed a sex worker named Jo-Jo around as though he didn't have anywhere to live. Pinkney thought I was just another addict on the block until one day, when I went from zero to a hundred. I went from trying to get two for eighteen or three for twenty-five dollars to selling quarter and half kilos of pure powder—not cooked up, but powder the hustlers could stretch with comeback and get paid double or quadruple their initial investment. This turnaround occurred a year after I moved off the block.

The thing is, I knew what the neighborhood hustlers did not know. I knew where to get a kilo of cocaine for two thousand dollars; I knew people who smuggled it from South America to Eleuthera, who owned twin-engine planes and cigarette boats, who transported no less than fifteen hundred pounds a haul. I knew people who worked on the docks in Miami, like Craig's father, who was running one hundred bricks a month to Gary's connection in DC. I knew things Pinkney and all the other young hustlers on T could never know because they limited themselves to the block they called their turf—a turf that nobody on

T Street could own or pay a mortgage to own, a turf that would fertilize its concrete soil with their blood in a heartbeat.

The question was, how did William D. Baker, Eric T. Franklin, Jamal R. Sampson, and Bryant C. Woodland know that ten kilos would be at 1303 T Street? This mystery was solved when the detective handling the case testified that the young men had spoken to a woman named Shorty, who told them about the cocaine and twice advised them to "go ahead and take it." After the second "go ahead and take it," they knew what to do. I knew the woman mentioned in court documents as Shorty. I met her when she was the side chick to Craig, who was married at the time.

When Craig's wife found out he was two-timing with Shorty, she pulled out a gun in their bedroom and almost shot the shit out of him. If I had not come into the bedroom and talked her out of it, he may have gone down. I had been to Shorty's house with Craig, staying a few days with whatever woman I brought, and we all snorted coke and hung at the after-hours joint on 9th Street. Shorty was slick as chicken grease, had a brickhouse body and plenty of street game, and could hustle her ass off.

During the time I was locked up, Gary and Craig had a huge falling-out after years of friendship, and Gary started dating Shorty behind Craig's back. Shorty played both ends to get to the money in the middle.

As for the falling-out, each side has a different version of the story, and I am torn as to which one to believe.

I heard Gary's version while I was still at Seven Locks. Gary was also at Seven Locks, having turned himself in, and was facing federal charges in the DC-Maryland-Virginia area. He was being held temporarily in the state of Maryland, so our time together was brief.

Gary was charged with conspiracy and conspiracy to distribute three hundred pounds of powder cocaine over a three-year period. He was also originally charged with wounding William D. Baker in the neck, but that charge was later dropped by the prosecutor in DC. Gary told me all of this while we sat in the same day room where I saw the original news story about the T Street incident on television. My longtime friend swore up and down in his blue jumper and flip-flops that Craig was the mastermind behind the attempted robbery because he was jealous of Gary. According to Gary, Craig fell out of favor with his dad (Bobby from Miami) after a series of fuckups, and he lost access to the coke coming up I-95.

I heard Craig's version of the story later, while living on West Virginia Avenue in Northeast DC after serving prison time and completing a rehabilitation program in Durham, North Carolina, as an alternative to incarceration. Craig was sleeping on my sofa at the time and working as a tow-truck dispatcher for a company in Arlington, a job I helped him get after I had been hired. When I asked him what happened, Craig told me a very different story. In his version, Gary had tried to drive a wedge between Craig and his father by revealing confidential information that Craig had trusted Gary not to tell. Craig was convinced that Gary started dating Shorty to make him jealous.

Craig insisted that Shorty played Gary, made him feel she was all about him, when in fact, she was waiting for the right moment to kill him.

I believe that the truth lies somewhere between these two versions. Either way, David was stabbed, Pinkney died pleading for his life on his knees, John lost the house his dad deeded to him, and Gary was sentenced to fifteen years in federal prison. Noticeably absent from the DC court documents is the name Bombshell, or Leon Dunham, as his mother named him, who had escaped the house that night. His name isn't redacted or blotted out to conceal his identity. He doesn't exist on paper and is still the invisible man he became long ago on the streets. We first met in a drug den on T Street about six months after I became homeless. That evening I had planned on walking to the Greyhound bus station to pick up a bus ticket my dad prepaid for me to come home.

After we smoked what little coke I had, Bombshell shared what he had with me. Maybe he knew that I was a fish out of water, that I didn't belong but acted like I belonged, or maybe he knew that the streets were mean but refused to let them take away his humanity. His offer to share was the ultimate sign of friendship on the streets. In return, I asked him to walk with me to the bus station, where I picked up my ticket and gave it to him to sell, which he did for ninety bucks to a complete stranger. We walked back up to T Street and continued doing what addicts do. Bombshell became a mentor, showing me where to find the shelters and free food, where to shower—how to appear normal when, in fact, I was not. If not for him, the streets might have devoured my will to live.

Ten years later, after obtaining a BA in DC, an MFA in Chicago, and a PhD in New York, I saw Bombshell on 14th Street hanging out in front of an auto parts store.

He was nodding on some form of opioid, probably China white. Bombshell was a creature of habit, apparently unaware of the gentrification of his surroundings, but he perked up when he saw me pulling over to the curb. I got out of the car, and we hugged and dapped up, the memories bobbing from a distant shore like a message in a bottle. "Everything happened in a split second," he said after the embrace. From "trying to get sleep" to "pop-pop-pop-pop-pop-pop" to "the slices into Dave's flesh" and then "opening the window" onto the roof and then "jumped, wasn't no time to think, had to get ghost"—I could tell that the posttraumatic stress wouldn't let Bombshell articulate this retelling without living the nightmare all over again in broad daylight.

The people who occupy 1303 will never know the complete backstory of that house, that block, that time in DC history.

What used to be familiar is now strange. Gentrification changes everything but the memory. If I close my eyes, I can visualize sitting with Andy, Joe, Lilton, Dwayne, Rock Steady, Bombshell, and Tonio under the tree after working day-labor jobs, digesting the day with a pint of vodka, dipping down in the basement vestibule to smoke coke, then coming back up as if the weight of the world had been lifted, if only for a moment. I can still picture Mr. Woody, sitting on his front porch and watching the cars drive by or the addicts going into 1425 to cop while grandkids danced to go-go music in front of the Gregorys' house.

Andy died from AIDS in 1992, and Lilton did the same three years earlier. Joe entered a drug program in 1991 and never got high again. Tonio was shot and killed in 1993, the same year Dwayne moved to Cleveland to escape the streets of DC and was never heard from again. Rock Steady contracted the virus that causes AIDS in 2001, when treatment ensured he would live longer than his friends. As with Bombshell, the opioids still have Rock Steady in suspended animation.

When I open my eyes again, I see that the corner store run by Ethiopians is still there. The Catholic Worker, next to 1303, is still there, a place where homeless people can get food, money, and clothes so that they can look for jobs.

But I also see that there is a new reality, one that tells me life is a continuum that enters and exits a narrative, snaking around corners, through dark tunnels, over bridges. Each stop a destination, each destination a place of embarkation.

Three Strikes and a Back Stab

In my parents' home there is a 1974 photo of an all-Black Catholic elementary school football team whose players don gold jerseys with black lettering and white pants.

Most of the eighth graders in the picture grew up attending the YMCA on 4th Avenue North, where we learned to butterfly, backstroke, flutter, and sidekick in the shallow end of the swimming pool. Danny Boy, Ralph, Cedric, Bo, and I went to summer camp outside Birmingham's city limits, playing tunk, spades, and bid whist on wooden picnic tables, the fresh pine cones scenting the warm Alabama air. We slammed dominoes, canoed the fresh water of Lake Logan Martin, and fished for bluegill and smallmouth bass off the lone pier. We rode Shetland ponies and minibikes through long, winding dirt trails as if race didn't matter in the city in which we lived. Nobody in the photo worried about what it meant to be Black because our parents had told us at an early age, "You are Black and beautiful," and the gaze through which we negotiated society was the Black one, not the white one. The photo represents a snapshot of history, a marker after which the realities of life came fast and sudden. Little did we know, in our youthful naïveté, that cocaine would wreck our lives during the '80s and well into the '90s.

Danny Boy's shiny Black skin and slim frame would be gunned down in a crack house as he tried to pass off demos as the real thing.

I would reconnect with Ralph in 1990 in the Brickyard, also known as Ensley Projects, smoking crack with my then-girlfriend, Donna. Cedric, nephew to Eddie Kendricks of the Temptations, would die of a brain aneurysm while I was incarcerated in 2000. I always circled back, though, to the kid kneeling next to me in the frame—Bo—and how I betrayed our friendship, how, to save his life, I had to stab my childhood friend in the back, the metaphorical bloodstain remaining on my hands to this day. The pain stems from Bo's not knowing the lengths I had to go to keep him walking upright and breathing, even though some would say he deserved what he got.

Bo and I attended the historic A. H. Parker High School, which opened its doors in 1900 and was one of the first all-Black high schools in the South.

In 1946, because of its large enrollment, Parker became known as the largest high school for Blacks in the world. The influential people who attended the school reads like a Who's Who in sports and the arts—Sun Ra, Nell Carter, Buck Buchanan, Lee May, and Erskine Hawkins, to name a few. Bo and I stayed in contact after graduation as we moved on into full-blown adulthood. He eventually came to visit me after I moved to Washington, DC, in 1986. By this time, I had dropped out of Howard and was working as a mail clerk on 19th and L Street while trying to be a player in the burgeoning drug game of the '80s. Cocaine was something most of my friends did not and could not escape. Some tried it, never to do so again; others continued chasing a white ghost, traveling down various roads that would lead them through an unavoidable hell on earth. It would be a few years before I made my way to Eleuthera and met JC, a drug runner for the South American cartels.

At the time, I dealt with my homeboy Big Fred, whose father was in New York, being supplied indirectly by the queen of narco-trafficking, Griselda Blanco.

I began dealing with Big Fred after the murder of my friend Jesse, whose girlfriend found his body—with seven bullet holes in his face—submerged in a bathtub full of water along with a plugged-in iron. Big Fred's father received shipments from a Colombian man driving a rented U-Haul stacked from floor to ceiling with bricks of cocaine. He fronted his son large quantities of cocaine, and Big Fred kept me supplied. When Bo came to visit, he saw firsthand how cocaine closed the gap between the haves and the have-nots. In this story, make no mistake, the protagonist is Bo and the tragic setting is Birmingham by way of Eleuthera and Miami.

To describe the triangular nature of this tale I need to go back to 1987 and a fateful meeting at a blackjack game in Los Angeles run by Otha Taylor, known as OT.

This meeting would eventually bring large shipments of narcotics to Birmingham, making OT one of the most prominent drug suppliers in the city. Along with OT came a crew of sidemen who saturated the streets with product. I knew how to glide low in a twin-engine plane, have dummy engines filled with kilos of cocaine, and strap a person with coke from head to toe as he or she strolled through US Customs. Yet OT was somebody I steered clear of when I came home to visit. I had met OT but decided I would not do business with him because I knew that one day he would land in prison.

Bo's saga began after I returned home from Washington, DC, in 1990, having lost the cocaine empire I tried to create in the late '80s and then fallen into the clutches of addiction.

After a couple of months in Birmingham, I caught up with Bo and found out that he had received a huge monetary settlement when the Volvo he rode in hit a cow in Tuskegee, Alabama. At the time of impact, Bo was hanging out of the sunroof, whistling at a girl. He needed to be airlifted to the nearest hospital, where doctors stapled his stomach back together. After a series of fuckups by Bo, his mother held a twenty-four-hour vigil over the settlement money, tightening his access to it and refusing to fuel his spending habits and addiction. The fuckups often occurred after he smoked too much cocaine. One of the ironies in this narrative is that our protagonist used some of the settlement money to buy the same Volvo model he'd been riding in during the collision. And because I had lost everything, I was willing to entertain the idea that Bo proposed in his living room. He would pawn his car for ten thousand dollars so that we could travel to the Bahamas and secure at least two kilos of powder from my connections, because both of us wanted—no, both of us needed—to make money.

The one person I knew in Birmingham who could lend Bo the money and hold his car as collateral was Wayne Poole.

On April 12, 1988, OT was arrested after an undercover investigation by the Alabama attorney general's office. According to the *Birmingham News*, at the time of OT's arrest he laid claim to being one of the "biggest dealers in the Birmingham area, perhaps the southeast region of the United States." Because Wayne associated with OT, he stepped into the kingpin role and oversaw distribution to the Loveman's Village projects and most of Smithfield. Wayne was my brother's friend, and I knew him well enough to ask him to lend the money to Bo in exchange for the car. In return, we would not only reimburse Wayne but give him seven ounces of cocaine for his trouble, which he didn't need; I also knew that

Wayne wanted to tap into my connection, perhaps break away from the West Coast influence, so I led him to believe that this might be a possibility.

With the financials for the trip secured, Bo found a woman to smuggle the product through customs, and we agreed to pay her two ounces for the risk.

The trip to Eleuthera began at the Birmingham airport, where we took a plane to Miami International, then boarded a twin-engine aircraft to fly over the dark blue Atlantic. Instead of landing on the northern tip of Eleuthera at Lower Bogue, we glided into the central township of Tarpum Bay. Because I didn't know how long it would take Zendel, my connection in Tarpum Bay, to hook up the deal, I told Bo not to secure a return ticket to Birmingham yet; we would handle that once we returned to Miami.

My first mistake: I should not have left Bo and the woman alone for the night while I drove an hour north to Hatchet Bay, catching up with my old friend Ben Delancey, but I did.

When I headed back down Queen's Highway to Tarpum Bay the next morning, I learned that Bo and the woman had discovered someone selling rocks and spent all our travel money in one night, smoking coke out of an aluminum can crowned with cigarette ashes. Bo probably would have tapped into the cop money we were going to use to buy the drugs had I not taken it with me in case I ran into JC on the island. The loss of the travel money created a desperate problem, and we had to figure out how to get back to Birmingham. Zendel found us a kilo of cocaine by day three for five thousand dollars. We departed the same day with cocaine strapped to the woman, strategically positioned and held in place with a girdle. There could only be one plan on how to get back to Alabama. Sure, I was totally beyond pissed at Bo for his foolish behavior, but I figured that we could still make the trip work.

The plan was to stay at my old college roommate's house in northwest Miami on 129th Terrace and have his brother, Keith, help sell some of the product so that we could get home.

My second mistake: I decided to pay my old friend Rudy a visit while marooned in Miami.

When I had met Rudy on spring break a decade before, he operated a base house, meaning his home was a place one could come and buy ready rock, smoke it through one of a hodgepodge of dirty glass pipes filled with cocaine residue that lined the closet shelves, and, if so inclined, go behind the kitchen door and choose from an assortment of women who would provide sexual pleasure for cash or product. Rudy was glad to see me, and he welcomed Keith and me in so that we could cook up two ounces and sell rock on 22nd Avenue, a busy thoroughfare of shop-and-cop traffic. We would not make much profit because Miami was the cheapest place to buy cocaine in the States (other than California) at the time. While we were out selling coke on the strip hand-to-hand to cars driving up, watching out for the stickup boys and the police, I left Bo at Rudy's house. Because Keith once broke into his mother's house to steal and sell the air conditioner in the dead of summer for cocaine, I needed to watch Keith just as much, if not more, than the police. When we returned from 22nd, Bo was stuck in a bedroom with three women and didn't come out for hours, smoking close to two ounces with the women in an all-out orgy. While I was gone, Rudy had to prevent Bo from being jacked twice.

Those same women Bo was partying with wanted to rob him and tried desperately to sneak out of the house and contact a group of stickup boys in the neighborhood.

Immediately after Bo emerged, I knew we needed to get out of the house before those girls did or we would most surely get robbed. In less than ten minutes a taxi was taking us back to Keith's mother's house, where I spent the night sleeping with one eye open to make sure Bo did not do anything else to jeopardize our situation. Early that next morning, Keith borrowed a car, and we made our way to Miami International Airport. I paid cash for two tickets to Birmingham for Bo and the woman, who had grown weary of the back and forth. But with the promise of five thousand dollars in profit off the two ounces she would be able to sell, she held on a bit longer.

I made my way to the Greyhound bus station, then copped a one-way ticket to Birmingham and held on to what was left of the kilo.

My third mistake: I met Bo back in Birmingham and gave him the package because, after all, it was his Volvo on the line as well as his money. At this point we were down to twenty-five ounces out of thirty-three and still needed to give Wayne seven ounces plus ten thousand dollars, which meant that our profits would amount to almost nothing. Then Bo disappeared. For two days I sat on pins and needles, then initiated the inevitable. I went to see Wayne to explain the situation, which he did not want to hear. "Product, money, or somebody's life, in any order," was his response. I didn't want Bo to die, but I knew Wayne would pump holes in his chest because he also told me, "I'll kill that nigga if I don't get my money."

After hearing the word *kill*, the solution to this problem became evident, and it would necessitate betraying Bo in order to save him.

When Bo finally called, I told him not to worry about the losses, that we could sell what we had left, fly back down to the Bahamas, perhaps double the money, and still come out on top. Meanwhile, I convinced a friend, Darnell, to stage a setup at his house. Darnell would pose as the broker, and another friend of mine, Jesse, would be the purchaser, along with one of his friends.

When Bo entered Darnell's house, I was already there, seated on the sofa, drinking cognac, and snorting lines of coke. Darnell welcomed Bo and seemed genuinely excited that he would be the middleman and make a nice chunk of change off the transaction. During our conversation, Jesse kicked in the front door, and he and his so-called accomplice drew their guns and gave us a look that said, *We ain't playing with you muthafuckas*. Bo froze, and if they were giving out Academy Awards, I would have gotten one for best actor. Jesse and his friend commandeered the package that Bo had laid on the table, ran out of the house, and hopped into a blue pickup truck. Before they could put the truck in drive, Darnell, sensing he might get left out of the split that would occur later, also ran out of the house and then dove into the flatbed of the truck, leaving Bo and me behind.

In the end, Wayne got his cut *and* kept Bo's Volvo. Darnell and the mock robbers received their cut, and I took the remaining product and moved back to Washington, DC, to restart my life.

I never considered the guilt that would accumulate over the years, each layer of shame building on the previous one.

The hidden wound of guilt never heals, never creates a scab. It lingers and festers. I twisted the knife in my friend's back when I knew he wrestled with a power greater than himself; the pain within me is everlasting and never ends. Bo would not be the last person I stabbed in the back, but I often rationalize the setup because his life hung between the living and the would-be-dead, a delicate calibration where one slight alteration either way would dictate the outcome. I could rationalize and tell myself he deserved it and believe it. What would a true friend do?

I sought to push the scales in favor of the living, knowing the drastic consequences that came with the decision.

Five years ago, while walking through aisle eleven at the Walmart in Birmingham, looking for deodorant and toothpaste because I had left them behind in the haste of packing and trying to catch an early flight from LaGuardia, I walked right into Bo. It was as if he had been stuck in time: his youthful skin refused to age, and there were no gray hairs or salt-and-pepper beard.

Perhaps, I thought, it was a curse coming back to haunt me: time had eaten away at my youth while Bo was allowed to be forever young. Then I heard a familiar voice from behind: "What up, Randall?" and I turned to see the version of Bo that correlated with the time gone by. The older Bo came around and stood beside the younger version so that both of them were facing me. The silence was deafening. I wondered if Bo knew what actually happened that night; after the incident, I had left him in Darnell's house to figure out the rest of his life. This was our first time seeing each other since then, and I wanted to tell him what happened, but the shame would not let me. This was not the conversation I wanted to have in the presence of Bo's son. While I stood mute, unable to speak to my childhood friend, he extended his right hand and hugged me with his left arm as if nothing had happened all those years ago.

Florida Turnpike via 6th and Chesapeake

Carl, Clarence, and I had hoped for an uneventful drive on the Florida Turnpike to Miami in our late-model Toyota, but we were unsure what to expect.

Given our youthful facial features, we could easily have been on spring break from college, looking to hang out on the beach and perhaps meet beautiful women. Our aim was not a pleasure trip, however, and we knew how the police and state troopers profiled young men like us. What the three of us wanted was a slice of the so-called American dream, and for us that meant buying powder cocaine at dirt-cheap prices, then reselling the commodified product to make a profit.

If capitalism had truly provided a free market, we wouldn't have trekked down this path. But we as Black men came from a long line of people denied equal participation in an economy fueled by the white bloom of cotton, an economy whose main participants were not compensated at all; our generation felt left behind, and we wanted to make up for what was lost through racism, slavery, segregation, and redlining with our own white bloom.

The drive from one Magic City to the next (that is, Birmingham to Miami) turned out to be uneventful after all. We arrived at a single-family home painted rust brown with green trim on 129th Terrace in northwest Miami and rang the doorbell. Craig Davis, my old roommate at Howard who had introduced me to the sale of cocaine, let us in. The goal of this trip was for Carl to purchase four ounces of powder from Craig; in return, Craig would split the two thousand dollars in profit he made and front me a couple of ounces to make more money.

This happened in the summer of 1984, three years before I began smuggling cocaine out of the Bahamas to Washington, DC, and Birmingham.

It took less than an hour for Craig to reach his father, Bobby, who, after having worked on the Miami docks for more than twenty years, was responsible for moving hundreds of pounds of cocaine and marijuana up and down the I-95 corridor. We were lightweights to Bobby, but the father always looked out for the son, and the son was my best friend from college. In this particular deal, I operated as middleman; Clarence was a childhood friend of mine, and he put Carl and me in contact, hoping to get a cut any way he could from the transaction. Carl originally did not want the powder Bobby brought because of the lack of dense rocks in the package—he wanted something less powdery. Bobby left and returned with a solid slab of rock weighing four ounces on the triple beam.

What I knew and Carl didn't was that all Bobby did was drive around the corner, take the product wrapped in plastic, and roll over it with his car tire, compressing the powder back into a solid mass. When Bobby returned, Carl seemed ecstatic at the huge mass. Since this was a cop and turnaround, in no time the three of us were back on the turnpike headed to Atlanta, where I had picked up both Carl and Clarence off I-20 East on the way to Miami. As I drove, the bright sun prepared to descend into evening, the traffic was sparse, and the drone from the tires provided our soundtrack. All at once I looked to my right and stared into the barrel of a .38 that Carl had pointed at my temple. Then, and only then, did I become aware of a potential problem with the deal that went down a couple of hours earlier.

Without moving the gun barrel, Carl announced, "Dude, you must think I'm a damn idiot. This package ain't right. I oughta bust a cap in yo' muthafuckin' ass right now."

Because I was driving, my eyes zigzagged from the gun barrel to the road. Clarence, who a minute ago seemed half asleep, was now fully awake. He told Carl, "Yo, man, what the hell's wrong with you? Don't do that. Ain't nobody tried to get over on you. Come on, dude." It was hard to tell whether Clarence didn't want the inside of the car splattered with brain matter and blood or whether he actually valued the years we had known each other in Birmingham, how we came of age skipping school, smoking weed, and drinking beer in his parents' basement. "Keep driving," Carl told me, and I did. At that point I realized I was being held hostage inside a car and began to ponder life and death instead of taking in the scenery or thinking about the potential payday.

If there was truth in the adage that everything happens for a reason, then Carl provided the reason, a point of reference, one I would draw upon two years later in my apartment in Southeast Washington, DC, in my dealings with Champ and Vido, both from Memphis.

I knew Champ better than Vido through a mutual friend, Dollar Bill, also from Memphis, whom I hustled with on campus before dropping out of school. Champ seemed like a little brother because he was three years younger; he had recently dropped out and was working at a car rental shop in what was then called National Airport, later renamed after a president who helped usher in the War on Drugs.

Champ didn't sell drugs but liked to be around the action, and I tried to look out for him whenever I could. I knew Vido's older brother a bit, and since Vido was a friend of Champ's, I let Vido hang around.

On the night in question, Champ and Vido were in my kitchen, watching me engage in the time-consuming process of breaking down a half-kilo of powder into amounts weighing sixteenth, eighth, quarter, and a full ounce. My pager beeped and flashed the number belonging to Hickie, my most trusted confidant and a person I'd grown up shooting marbles with between the shotgun houses in Smithfield. After talking with Hickie on the phone, I asked Champ and Vido to drive over to Hickie's place on 6th and Chesapeake to drop off an ounce. Hickie knew that before the night was over he would run out of product, and we both didn't want to miss out on any money.

I knew Hickie's mother, Dot, very well. Dot was my grandmother's righthand woman and helped raise me in the bootleg house on 127 8th Avenue North.

Hickie graduated from A. H. Parker High School in 1978, a year before me, and we didn't have any contact for seven years until I ran into him by chance at a liquor store on South Capitol Street in Washington, DC. During our conversation I learned that Hickie controlled a section of 6th and Chesapeake in Southeast, selling powder for purchasers to cook up in a beige ball, place in a stem, and fascinate over a tornado swirl of smoke that would beam them up into an uncharted galaxy. Hickie experimented with ready rock long before crack became the street standard.

From that day forward, we Birmingham boys built a business in Southeast, with me fronting packages that would allow for Hickie to compensate his workers nicely and make a profit as well. Hickie could sell enough in small quantities to flip three to four ounces a day on Chesapeake, a hotspot well known for its around-the-clock activity. Between the time Champ and Vido left my house and the next morning when Hickie called, I assumed the package had been dropped off, and the 3.5 grams I gave Champ and Vido seemed well worth the profit I would make. But when Hickie began the conversation with "What happened?" instead of "Good morning," and told me that no one had shown up at his house last night, I knew something in the milk wasn't clean. Hickie and I had a problem.

The drive from Hickie's place to mine usually took about thirty minutes, but Hickie made it in twenty. Under his windbreaker was a tan shoulder holster with a .357, and after he sat down on the living room couch, I could see the rage in his clenched teeth. He expressed how particularly upset he was about the money he missed out on Friday night because of the lack of product. I wasn't in this game to harm people or kill them, but at that point I didn't see how I could protect Champ and Vido. Hickie and I sat in silence, doing a couple of lines of blow, until the phone rang. It was Champ. "Man, can I talk to you, Homeboy?" he asked in a humble tone, indicating that he'd fucked up and wanted my sympathy. He told me that Vido's brother, who was a construction contractor in the city, promised to pay for the package that they had smoked overnight at Champ's sister's house in Southwest DC.

On one hand, I could empathize with Champ, having been in his position before. I knew the triggering effect that comes from watching a white cloud of smoke funnel through a glass bowl after a beige rock is lit by a butane torch. I could replicate in my subconscious how the medicinal smoke numbed the body, and for a moment—an almost infinite space between the past and the present—one could be in paradise, only to feel the euphoria fade and be unable to stop the mad chase to recapture it, disregarding reason and practicality for a pipe dream.

The inner consciousness sells an unobtainable dream, a nonexistent mirage, and every pledge to repay the money you will never be able to come up with is a lie compounded into eternal hell when the fog clears from the brain. I asked Champ where Vido was, and he informed me that his friend was at Slowe Hall, the off-campus Howard University dorm in the LeDroit Park section of Northwest DC.

On the other hand, I was sure Champ knew that my homeboy would not be as compassionate as I would be, even if we all were from the South. I decided to protect Champ and offer Vido as the sacrificial lamb.

When I retold this event years later to a group of poets at a major creative writing conference, I was met with gasps and utter disbelief.

These poets had won every kind of national recognition you could think of—the Pulitzer Prize, National Endowment for the Arts Fellowships in Literature, the Whiting Award, the National Book Critics Circle Award, Guggenheim Fellowships. They had all attended the right Ivy League schools, and their life trajectories did not include drugs and violence. Over drinks at a hotel bar, I explained how Hickie, though he had never set foot on a college campus, went to Slowe Hall at 1919 3rd St. NW, because I was protecting Champ, and Dollar Bill would never forgive me if something happened to his friend. Hickie brought foot soldiers unafraid to do the dirty work, and parked in front of the dorm, watching the flow of hopeful students who expected to earn college degrees and embark on successful careers as doctors, lawyers, actors, pharmacists, teachers, and business executives.

Although Hickie attended an all-Black high school, I doubt he knew that Lucy Diggs Slowe was the first Black woman in the country to serve as dean of women at a university; or that she was one of the sixteen founders of the first Black sorority, Alpha Kappa Alpha; or that her long-time housemate, Mary Burrill, was really her romantic partner, a woman greatly respected by writers and poets during the Harlem Renaissance. No, Hickie couldn't have cared less about this period of Black history, commemorated by the building where Vido was holed up. Hickie did see the ambition in these students' faces, but he couldn't have cared less about their intended professions; instead, he singled out one gullible student, who gave up Vido's room number in the belief that Hickie was a cousin from out of town.

Hickie and his foot soldiers climbed the stairs to the second floor. Hickie pulled the .357 out of its holster and knocked on the door.

When Vido answered, he damn near shit his pants. Hickie and his foot soldiers marched Vido down two flights of stairs, through the main entrance, and into the car, the busy traffic of Howard University students unaware that hidden under the windbreaker draped over Hickie's arm was a gun pressed to Vido's spine. The car took off and headed toward 6th and Chesapeake to Hickie's apartment. The foot soldiers strapped

Vido in a chair, and Hickie gave him twenty-four hours to come up with the money for the package he had smoked up plus the profit missed. When Hickie called me to relay what had occurred, I knew that death was a very real outcome, so I climbed into my red convertible and drove to Hickie's apartment to survey the situation. Once there I saw Vido begging for help, telling me that all he needed to do was make one call to his brother, who would (for the love of family) find a way to get him out of this situation. Thankfully for Vido, Hickie needed the money more than he needed a corpse.

Maybe because Hickie's mother, Dot, and my grandmother, Rosie Lee, were best friends, Hickie didn't shoot Vido on the spot.

The sight of Vido strapped to a chair, pleading for help, snapped me back to that car ride in 1984 on the Florida Turnpike when I was held at gunpoint. Memory is often triggered by an emotion, an event, or some situation that you've tried to suppress deep within the recesses of your mind. In the vortex of my memory, it wasn't that I was pleading for my life: begging always indicates weakness, and I couldn't be perceived as feeble if longevity in the game was my goal. Instead, I had decided to determine my own fate by reasoning with Carl. I asked him to remember the events leading up to our copping the drugs, walked him through each one of them, and asked what would make him think I was trying to cheat him. Did he not get a solid rock? Did he not pay a fair price? Did I not do what I said I was going to do? Was the cocaine not pure? Did anyone rob him?

With that said, there is still a helplessness associated with a .38 pointed at your skull. Being held at gunpoint destroys any misconceptions about life's longevity. You also begin to think about God and what happens after one is physically removed from the planet. Then there are the questions flashing inside the eyelids: What is on the other side? Will I have an awareness of the life I left? Is everything connected? Are human beings fragmented, contorting and constantly reassembling themselves throughout infinity?

By the time we reached the other side of Orlando, entering Kissimmee, the pure raw power of the coke Carl snorted seemed to be wearing off. When Carl put the gun away and apologized, I didn't have the awareness or the knowledge of what would happen in the future, how this event would perhaps save a life, because it did.

I took Hickie into the bedroom, calming him down to the point that he agreed to wait on Vido's brother to pay nearly four thousand dollars for this nightmare to be over. Vido's body would not be found in Charles County, Maryland, in the back of a stolen car set on fire. I also didn't know poetry would be in my future, and that my past would create a way in which I could support myself through language, or that I would have a literary career and retell segments of this story to award-winning writers whose lives had been very different from mine. While taking I-20 West from Atlanta, the only thing I wanted to imagine was a beautiful sun slowly falling over a horizon of pine trees in Birmingham, and to be thankful for another day among the upright.

Archetypes and Disaster

The women who worked as transportation specialists, a term I prefer to the derogatory *mules*, almost always lived below the poverty line. Without question, these brave souls could spit in the face of fear without a second thought. To succeed in this risky line of work, a woman had to possess a strong hunger for a slice of that elusive American pie, had to be able to exit a twin engine in Miami strapped head to toe with a white powder that had taken American society by storm, ride the shuttle to the monorail, and then stroll through US Customs wrong as two left shoes but still walking like she owned the place. She needed to make declarations to the waiting agent without a nervous twitch, and then blend into the human fabric of the airport. If the job description were to appear in the classifieds or online job listings, it might read this way:

> One black or brown female wanted. Slightly addicted to cocaine but more addicted to the dollar-dollar bill. Able to wear the mask, existing as both correct and incorrect, and merge into mainstream corporate America. Needs to be hood on the inside but able to speak with perfect diction to people unable to code-switch and make decisions in the blink of the eye. Must, and this is important, possess the gift of gab and resent the capitalist nature of a government that has oppressed the applicant's lineage for 450 years or more, leaving the applicant unable to participate in a booming economy that promotes the greatest nation on the planet. Should be angry at a system that reduces the applicant to the invisible, inconsequential, and nonexistent.

Every time one of these specialists successfully reentered the United States, she was paid between fifteen hundred and two thousand dollars for each kilo wrapped around her body, depending on the going market rate in Eleuthera, Bahamas. This rate often fluctuated between fifteen hundred and five thousand dollars. Some women could carry more than others, depending on their body shape. The women I chose knew they were risking ten years of precious life and did so without regret, which speaks more to the human condition in which they lived. Imagine the desperation one must feel to risk freedom for a small measure of the happiness that makes one feel alive.

The prototype for this endeavor was a woman named Jo-Jo, who resided at 1325 T Street in the Northwest corridor of Washington, DC. Jo-Jo fit the job description in that her human condition was a socio-logical case study in systemic oppression and economic depravity. Her mother, a big-boned Anglo-Saxon from the hills of West Virginia with an eighth-grade education, married a stocky coal-black man from South-east Washington, DC. Needless to say, the family was hanging on to the bottom rung of society. This was Jo-Jo's inheritance: a stay-at-home mother and an underemployed father scrambling to keep the rent paid through odd construction and maintenance jobs. The family received food stamps, and when each daughter began to have children while still living in the household, the welfare checks became crucial to the family's survival. There were five girls and one baby boy. None of the girls made it past the tenth grade at Cardozo High School without getting pregnant and dropping out. This was their rite of passage into womanhood—the tenth grade seemed to mark the spot. When I met Jo-Jo she'd just turned twenty-one, two years removed from having her second daughter.

The first time I smuggled cocaine through US Customs, in 1987, I did it myself with the help of my brother. We broke down and wrapped half a kilo around our midsection, down our thighs, and up the crack of our ass. Baggy shorts and long XXL T-shirts had come in vogue, so this was our dress code as we cleared customs after an international flight. I knew, however, that this could not continue if I wanted to bring in larger shipments, which is where Jo-Jo entered the scene. By this time we were lovers, though I wouldn't say boyfriend and girlfriend, as least not yet. I knew I could convince her to take a chance as long as cocaine and money were involved. On our first Aero Coach trip together over the Atlantic from Miami, we hit an air pocket fifteen minutes out from Lower Bogue and dropped a hundred feet. Jo-Jo screamed at the top of her lungs, so loud the person next to her asked whether it was her first time flying. The pilot half chuckled at the sudden scream before apologizing to the eight passengers for the turbulence as we prepared to land on the tarmac.

The island men fell in love with Jo-Jo's bright biracial complexion, hazel eyes, and straight black hair. Her skin was dazzling in the sun, and the lusty distraction she provided allowed me to connect with suppliers and not worry about people asking why we were there. Jo-Jo quickly became a master of deception, walking through customs while looking regal and ice-water smooth. She could only carry one kilo at a time because of her small stature and body shape. Sometimes we flew to Eleuthera and back from Miami in a day, for the most part posing as a couple headed to our vacation home in Hatchet Bay from Washington, DC. Although Craig Davis, my old college roommate who started me in the game, was serving out the rest of a seven-year federal sentence for conspiracy to distribute in the state of Maryland, his mother would let me use the spare room in her Miami house whenever I was in town. Jo-Jo and I would make one trip, wait two days, then make another trip and then fly back to DC. Like I say, the girl was fearless.

Over time, along with being fearless, Jo-Jo became more addicted to cocaine, and I, at times, would binge with her, though I knew how to snap myself back to reality and become functional again. The one thing that never bothered me at the time, but has since come to haunt me, was her daughters. They were extremely young and needed their mother when I took her away for months at a time, living a fast life that risked a substantial prison sentence. I would give Jo-Jo money to take care of the kids, but they missed their mother and were destined to repeat the same cycle as their aunts. I know that with each passing year, their resentment toward me must have increased as they watched their mother deteriorate from drug abuse. In my mind, I thought I was helping at the time, but in reality, I was destroying the mother-daughter bond.

Because I loved Jo-Jo and knew our lives would be intertwined for years, I eventually made her stop transporting cocaine. This is when I began to search for someone else to pick up where Jo-Jo left off.

Pam, a young woman from Baltimore, was taller and had a more ample physique than Jo-Jo; she could carry three kilos wrapped around her body without the slightest hint that she might be transporting an illegal substance across international lines. The setup was always the same: we traveled as a couple, hand in hand, and stayed on the island until I secured the packages, then left the next day. Pam liked to party when she got to the island, so I would always have to sequester her in a private villa in the townships of Hatchet Bay, Governor's Harbour, or James Cistern while I took care of business.

On our eighth trip to the island, we stayed at Rainbow Inn, just outside Hatchet Bay, at the suggestion of my good friend Ben Delancey, whose daughter was married to my brother. Once we landed on the island, I went through my usual routine—visiting my connection, doing what I had to do, securing three kilos—only this time I decided we would stay an extra day since the inn sat on four beautiful acres and our cottage was immaculate.

Then there were the tranquil, deep-blue waters of the Atlantic that seduced the body to the point of lovemaking, which is exactly what Pam and I did for the first time. We were not a couple, and I didn't want to mix business with pleasure, but I got caught up in the moment.

The day before we were to leave, I was lying on the couch, looking at Pam, who was damn near butt-naked walking around the cottage, smoking coke out of a plastic bottle fitted with an ash bowl, the tube of an ink pen protruding from the side. I watched Pam open the sliding-glass door and head for the beach.

Between the cottage and the beach there was a patch of coral that had to be negotiated. Pam wasn't wearing sandals, and as she stepped on the coral barefoot, she immediately lost her balance. I saw her wobble as she tried to regain control, then fall, face first, into the coral. I leapt off the couch, running to where she had fallen, and when Pam rose, I saw potholes spread out over her face. I knew she needed to see a doctor immediately.

There was no telephone in the cottage—very few people possessed their own telephones at the time—so I scooped Pam off the jagged coral, brought her back inside, got her and myself dressed, and hopped into the car while she cried.

Driving north on Queen's Highway, I tried to convince Pam that her injuries weren't that bad. But when we arrived at my friend Ben's house in Hatchet Bay, he took one look at her and said, "Let me drive." There was no doctor in Hatchet Bay, and when we reached the bordering township of Gregory Town, the doctor had just left the island. By this time it was nightfall. Ben recommended putting antibiotic ointment on Pam's face and catching the first flight back to the States in the morning.

There was little doubt Pam needed a doctor, and I secretly wondered whether she'd ever be as beautiful as she was before the fall. When Pam woke up the next morning after trying to ease the pain with more drugs, she didn't look much better, but assured me she could do the job she came to do. I promised myself that this would be her last time. We then went through the ritual of breaking down the fiberglass-wrapped blocks that had made the trip from South America to Hatchet Bay.

I had never worried about going through customs with Jo-Jo or Pam, until now.

For the return trip to Miami, I decided that we'd switch airlines and fly Pro Air from North Eleuthera Airport. I had become friends with most of the workers there via Craig Davis and knew they would take good care of me; I also knew we could no longer blend into the crowd because Pam's face looked like it needed urgent medical attention. After we landed in Miami and took the shuttle to the monorail, things appeared to be going smoothly. We exited the rail, went up the escalator with our luggage, and got in line at customs. I felt an abrupt tap on my shoulder and worried that this was the trip that would land me in jail—not because I had cocaine on me, because I didn't, but Pam did, and we were traveling together. The customs agent pointed us to a table where we were instructed to place our luggage.

After we did so, another agent put on a pair of rubber gloves, opened my luggage, and proceeded to dig around the lining and under the clothes, squeezing socks, the heels of shoes, pants pockets, anything bulky. After going through my bags, he began the same process with Pam's. The agent thought he'd found the mother lode when he spotted an extra-large bottle of baby powder, but when he opened the top and squeezed, baby powder flew out and saturated the air, settling on our faces. Pam and I both wanted to laugh but were acutely aware of the three kilos hidden by the dark blue sundress she was wearing.

After the powder cleared the air, the agent finally focused on Pam's face, zeroing in on the craters punctured in her once-smooth skin.

I stepped in at this point to explain that we'd come back earlier than planned from Eleuthera because of the accident and lack of medical care on the island. I told the agent we had a small window to catch our connecting flight to DC, where we would go directly to George Washington Hospital. The agent turned his attention back to Pam, calculating the sum of each crater, the size of the stiches that would be needed, the pain and subsequent care before making the decision to let us pack up and be on our way.

The bullet we dodged at that moment was a hollow point, meant to inflict pain and possible death, all of which a prison sentence can do. We were allowed to pass through expeditiously to catch our flight. I took Pam to the hospital in DC after stopping by the house and dropping off the package. I never heard from Pam again after she left the hospital and went back to Baltimore.

Though Jo-Jo and Pam have different storylines, the two narratives meet and dialogue at the intersection of ruin, both theirs and mine.

I ultimately abandoned the idea of using a transportation specialist and figured out a different way to transport the drugs. I knew people who worked for Pro Air at North Eleuthera Airport, so I arranged to give one of them a suitcase filled with cocaine during baggage check-in. That person would personally put the bag on the twin engine bound for Miami, placing it together with the properly checked bags. In Miami another baggage handler, knowing the dimensions and color of the bag, would grab it off the plane, and, instead of putting it with the rest of the baggage to go through customs, would take it back to the hangar, hide it until quitting time, then bring it home for pickup. This became an efficient way to get the product back to DC to sell in a market already flooded by the drug kingpin Rayful Edmond III, whom I refused to work with because, as with OT in Birmingham, I knew Rayful was going to jail at some point, given the bodies of his associates that were piling up.

When this arrangement came tumbling down amid deception, jealousy, and greed, the impact was immediate. I had no time to brace for the whirlwind that was about to envelop me.

The first night I became homeless, I slept in an abandoned car in the back alley on 13th and T Street, behind Jo-Jo's house. The next morning, I had to learn how to survive in a city that was saturated with cocaine and whose homeless faction could be ruthless and uncaring. I crossed the city, staying at shelters from Northeast to Northwest DC while memorizing intake times so as not to be late and forgo an army cot for the night. Like an animal in the woods who learns where the food is and returns to that bountiful place to stay alive, I discovered So Others Might Eat (SOME), a place where I could get three meals a day, if need be, depending on where my travels took me. I found out the locations and serving times for the Martha's Table food wagon. I learned that the

Catholic Worker on 13th and T served dinner, and if I wanted a fancy meal, I could make the trek uptown to the borderline of Tacoma Park and Silver Spring, where an organization served home-cooked food. The hell I endured some nights sleeping inside the bus, train, or Metro station, on a park bench in Logan Circle, in the shelter at a bus stop, or in a seat at George Washington Hospital brought me to the point of hopelessness and despair.

The line of individuals I need to seek apologies from is long; it hugs the contours of city blocks and snakes around country farmland and through the Appalachian hills.

Every day since coming out of the fire, I've made it my life's mission to advocate for those in prison, constantly reiterating that there needs to be a pathway to reform and forgiveness. Digging through episodes of my life is like discovering undetonated bombs, and I try to handle each one carefully to avoid setting off explosions of remorse. Sometimes it's hard to forgive myself; I do ask forgiveness from others, though, in an attempt to balance the negative energy I put into this world with something positive. If I were to address that long line of people I have hurt, I might begin this way: Forgive the echoes of guilt and time's continuum, which refuses to erase a memory. Forgive the gun and the squeezed trigger. Forgive the falsehood of masculinity and the bullets penetrating the car window, missing a newborn in the back seat. Darkness cloaked us in its vice grip—forgive me, but I was blind. Forgive the attempted murder on 13th and Euclid; I didn't believe the penitentiary was a real and tangible place where the erased go to be forgotten amid the metal chatter of cell doors and keys, the click of black boot heels along the hall, and the bleak silence of the housing unit. Forgive the eyes at half-mast that I cultivated: the bottomless pits of screams and whys. Forgive me, for I could not see the ragged outline of myself, a broken piece of a human being, unable to be whole.

Forgive the fragmentation of this too-late apology and of every life I fucked up in the pursuit of selfishness.

A Day in the Life of Cell 23

Morning waits to emerge in Housing Unit III, C-Tier as I sit on a metal chair and contemplate, my back against a wall encasing a rectangular window slit.

Dawn and darkness dictate the governing themes outside this fortress in the farm hills of Hagerstown. On the metal desk in cell 23 that is bolted to the opposite wall, a yellow legal pad with blue lines functions as rehabilitation for crimes committed against the state of Maryland. An urban scene emerges from one single thought traced from memory with a clear plastic pen. Although written inside Roxbury Correctional Institution, the emerging story is set at the Clifton Terrace projects in Washington, DC, a place many outside the city limits would be surprised even exists. The protagonist is a true representation of actual victims, the unsuspecting Black man who tried to discover an alternative path to the good life by selling a drug—an idea dreamed up to eradicate and erase those who were never allowed to embrace the spirit of capitalism.

Unfolding on the pages of the pad: wet snowflakes descend intermittently from a sullen sky onto the oval courtyard of Clifton Terrace, a maze no rat could ever escape. Here, men and women are drawn to each other in back stairwells by vice and obsession. Here, where sometimes the air is filled with sulfur from the fumes of automatic weapons, flocks of seagulls pull themselves into a V while their droppings splatter on the hoopless blacktop. The sweet harmony of pickup games—the dribble, the behind-the-back-crossover-no-look-pass followed by the swish and the proverbial *You can't check me, Slim!* are gone until summer. The main character walks up the back stairwell of the triangular tenement, passing addicts mesmerized by plumes of pallid smoke pulled from a glass straight-shooter packed with Chore Boy and residue. Young Black men with grocery sacks full of dime bags magically appear on the landings, hoping to get rich and retire after selling a product that will soon have them dead or in jail doing a mandatory dime piece.

This is how the story begins before the metal doors roll back at 5:30 A.M. and the men of C-Tier stream out of their relegated cells to form one human mass.

The collective body of so-called felons, meaning those who will forever carry the stain of prison, walk in unison a hundred yards toward the dining hall to consume a breakfast of two boiled eggs, farina, white bread, and coffee. One of the meal servers is almost always accused of "shaking the spoon," or placing less rations on one receiving tray than on the others. No one gets shanked on the way back from breakfast, breaking a three-day stretch in which someone did indeed bleed on the concrete.

Though this small miracle occurs, the act will not be recorded in the annals of prison statistics. Up the walkway we proceed like cattle back into the housing unit and are locked in until count time. The first sunlight enters through the window slit, providing a glimpse of the heat that will envelop the unit by noon. When the guards come to my cell to count me present and accounted for, I have contextualized the main character in the story, who is barely sixteen and filled with a rage that emanates from a father who refused to recognize him as son.

In the story, the mother sells her body three hundred sixty degrees around Logan Circle, and the boy no longer views school as a viable option.

Bystanders at the elementary school on that fateful day would recount, *It was terrible how the teacher's two front teeth flew out of his mouth.* The social studies teacher, from Yale and then Teach for America, possessed no knowledge of street-corner ways, the young'uns clocking fifteen thousand dollars a clip with no taxes. When he told this young kid, who was involved in a soon-to-be-national narrative, to "please shut up," the teacher misunderstood the pressure, the plight of young melanin men gunned down in broad daylight—history, too, can be a mean bitch. On Chesapeake Avenue, the tone of voice used by the teacher in his bold request to please shut up unequivocally meant at least a two-piece to the jaw; hence, the teacher's two front teeth flew out of his mouth. Nothing could save do-gooder Yale from the young kid's fists, which really wanted to reply, *I'm still a dream, someone save me.* But no one did, and our main character rationalizes life on the streets as the only way to rise above his human condition.

The shakedown in the cells occurs unannounced and begins with one of three guards dismantling my bunk, searching for metal objects with the potential to puncture.

One guard eyes the yellow pad with my uncompleted story and the books lined on the metal table, notably *The Autobiography of Malcolm X*, *Convicted in the Womb*, *Makes Me Wanna Holler*, and *Maud Martha*. The story and the books are raked off the desk onto the floor in one swoop. I am asked to pick the books up and shake them by the spine to ensure nothing is lodged between the pages—but there is language hidden between the pages, words helping me break free of cell 23. The weapons I am using to escape are hidden in the open, disregarded as collectible bulk, and for a brief moment I am winning this constant battle against time.

When the doors open, I exit and take a left, walk five cells down, then make another left into the day room to conduct my daily fellowship with Big Pun, who grew up in east Baltimore and is nursing a nickel for possession with intent to distribute, and Hell Naw from Southeast DC, who is one year into a three-year bid for credit card fraud, along with Sebastian, who grew up in Takoma Park and is walking down a mandatory ten for possession of .28 grams of crack cocaine. Each day we relive the memories left behind through a dialogue in the past tense, talking about the things we *used to do*.

Because the hillbilly white boy from Maryland Eastern Shore is new, he doesn't understand the unwritten rules of the day room or the unwavering sentiment of C-Tier, and he tries to change the television channel. The resulting slap is so pronounced, the occupants of the day room aren't sure if the sound emanated from the domino table or Milkman's cuffed hands. When Milkman slaps him a second time, the originating sound is confirmed. From this day forward—until the white man from Eastern Shore checks into protective custody—he will be placed on a mandatory fast by the occupants of C-Tier. Each of his meals will be confiscated by Milkman and Black, who pass out the trays three times a day.

By the time Big Pun finishes getting a tattoo of a naked lady drawn on his arm, with a tricked-out cassette player under the TV used to shield the illegal act, it is time for lock-in again.

I go back to cell 23, sit at the metal desk, and continue the story. The main character meets his drug connection on 13th and T Street, an older guy with a hookup to people in Florida who offer good prices.

The sixteen-year-old is given two ounces of crack and expected to give the man twenty-four hundred dollars, meaning there is a total profit to be had of twenty-six hundred dollars in a matter of three hours. At home in Garfield Terrace, under the sixteen-year-old's mattress, there is close to fifty thousand dollars earned in the past month. What the boy doesn't know is that the cocaine received from the man, in actuality, was worth five hundred dollars. The kilo it originated from was stretched with vitamin B12 and rerocked back into twelve hundred fifty grams, creating an extra quarter-kilo. In the story, I'm trying to show how easy it was for boys from challenging circumstances to see crack as a viable option among no options at all.

With the pen I retrace a narrative I know well from recall. I need to make sense of what I left behind on the streets, to adequately explain why so many boys and Black men are entering the vicious repetitive cycle that is prison. Before the doors roll back open I place the character outside the main gates of Clifton Terrace, which is only a few blocks from Garfield Terrace. The first rule he learns from the old head that sold him packages is not to hustle where you lay your head. The boy stands on the sidewalk with a grocery bag full of dime bags, selling to his friends' mothers and fathers, their sisters and grandmothers—call it a family affair. The goal is to buy his mother a single-family home in Silver Spring, to save her from the clutches of crack with a new environment so that the two of them could be a real family and prove that there was no need for the absentee dad.

When the doors roll back again, Sebastian meets me at the front of my cell, and we line up for outside rec.

Sebastian's legal appeals were long ago denied, and now he has no choice but to walk down the mandatory time. The woman he left behind in the streets will not come visit, let alone write a letter. He is holding on to a fading memory of her and refuses to forget the last sensation of meaningful touch he experienced. Because Sebastian didn't receive proper dental care when he arrived from the Department of Corrections, three of his front teeth are missing and he talks with a pronounced lisp. On this day I want to offer a lifeline to help Sebastian discover a little joy amid so much despair.

We head to the oval track, a soft dirt path paved with pebbles that crunch as Sebastian and I walk. I tell him I will write the letter to his girl, and he can copy and send it as if it were his own. By now, everyone in the block knows I can push the pen; after crafting a letter for a dude in cell 42 that drew a response from his girlfriend, I collected five Cup-a-Soups and two packs of Oodles of Noodles as payment and began writing other letters as a burgeoning side hustle. While we walk, the sun is almost at full strength, and on one of our turns on the oval track we place a hand over our eyes to shield them from the glare. Sebastian describes the letter he wants me to respond to: "She wanted me to hold her hand in public. Said I don't communicate. Wanted me to see her as a person, not a sexual object."

After Sebastian and I walk two miles, we see the violent nature of basketball on full display as we round a curve onto the straightaway.

Two men square off at the top of the key, after a hard foul followed by a "Fuck you, nigga" exchanged by both parties; neither man could care less about Black-on-Black crime. Because the fight occurs in the public sphere, no weapons are produced. They throw down like middleweight boxers until the guards rush in and break it up, escorting both men to the hole—solitary confinement. We keep walking, and the weight-lifting pit comes into view, with Milkman and Black bench-pressing iron on top of iron. Milkman played fullback for two years at the University of Maryland, dropped out when he realized that he could earn unbelievable money selling crack, then got caught and had to do the mandatory ten-year sentence.

Black never played any kind of sports—didn't even finish high school—but prospered in Baltimore selling large quantities of crack until he, too, became a mandatory-sentencing statistic.

Both men could be bodybuilders because of the extensive workouts they do each day. These guys are so huge it is abnormal, and no one dares challenge them unless he wants to get broken to pieces. We keep walking, and I can tell that Sebastian is in pain about his woman. Even though she has forgotten all about him, her lingering scent after seven years is all he has left. "I will write a letter," I tell him. "I needed to know these things if I am going to sound sincere. I will have it for you in the morning, typed up." The whistle blows, and we head back into the housing unit to shower and spend more time in the day room or stay in our cells until dinner.

Back in cell 23 there is the undeniable sound of keys pecking on a prison-approved electric typewriter purchased through commissary with a money order sent from Birmingham.

The typewriter is a way to earn extra commissary by typing writs, legal briefs, and any other documents that need to look professional. In prison, the list of people requiring this kind of service is long. I decide to stay in my cell after returning from dinner. The get-my-girl campaign for Sebastian begins before I go back to the story-in-progress. Letters like his are useful as warm-up exercises before I begin typing the work started early this morning, with edits and revision done in the evening, concluding with a typed-up version that will end the night.

I create a remembrance of love: the reasons the two hooked up, who made who laugh first, the first time they said, "I love you," and a renewed promise at the end to be a better and more vulnerable human being. The epistle of love I write for Sebastian is not that different from the others I write. Currently I am batting a hundred because each mailed letter has solicited a response, but I had to put in double work for Sebastian, looking in the dictionary and then flipping to the thesaurus to find the proper words to articulate his point of view. I will be totally surprised when his girlfriend writes back two weeks later. I will know because Sebastian will yell, "She wrote me!" from his cell on the top tier during mail call.

The sixteen-year-old protagonist is dead, robbed and then shot at point-blank range in front of Clifton Terrace.

There was no happy ending, only the dead boy's blood painting a tragic mural on the cold concrete sidewalk as the reflections of his life flickered in the setting sun. In the end, the story had to write itself out, the platinum chain of success wrapped around the boy's neck as he lay motionless, a bullet hole to the dome. I could not save my character from the history he was preordained to make, a protagonist manipulated by social powers in place since before his birth, each life-altering decision a pathway to a dead end. The sixteen-year-old is representative of the teenagers I left trying to outrun their environment. Unfortunately, as my brother says, ain't nobody mad but the folks that ain't getting none, and the fourteen-year-old who held the nickel-plated .357 Magnum and pulled the trigger had the same philosophy as the now deceased. Of course the story is autobiographical fiction—I do not write THE END because those words should not be the lasting images for my potential reader.

This is my daily routine in prison, and nothing changes in how I approach each day. Each person here helps build a collective image that is fed to the American public. Milkman and Black roll the ice cart around to each cell after 10:00 P.M. lock-in. Because Black discovered the Nation of Islam and found my college experience insightful during our many conversations, he is always talking about Black empowerment when he and Milkman appear in front of my cell at night. Even when we disagree, we always agree on self-determination within the Black community. Although Milkman doesn't say a word, he always listens intently, as if intrigued by Black's thought process. After we dap up and the guard closes my cell, the two resume what they will continue to do every night, seven days a week, three hundred sixty-five days a year. One of the wheels on the cart makes a rickety noise, an uneven repetition that sends everyone on C-Tier to sleep, and we will wake up tomorrow and do it all over again.

Reevaluation

It was the slow opening of April, before cherry blossoms bloomed on Constitution Avenue and lit the exit out of the city.

Uptown in an eight-block radius, avenues and streets demarcated the impending white bloom in America. Angel dust, or Love Boat (PCP), became a forgotten, beautiful high to a butt-naked, addicted fiend now in love with a drug decomposed to a beige rock: crack. The fiend pledged till-death-do-us-part or prison, whichever came first. A generation was trying to get paid in full before 1988's summer of love and, thereafter, casualties galore. Once-deadened leaves rematerialized on maple trees unable to block the perfume of July: sweltering heat plus a boy's decaying body in the alley behind O Street Market, lying faceup in rigor—his pockets inside out, not one red cent left after the jack and subsequent murder. Can you imagine a lost city?

Reimagine what you know: the beloved father strung out on freebase, listening to go-go music, addicted to bass: Trouble Funk, EU, and Chuck Brown. Base on every street corner begetting death. Addicted to the image, we got base before a two-piece and mumbo sauce, before asylum, before love. Base, then ready rock, then crack, then death. Being "real" became fashionable, the baseball bat, another weapon for us base heads. Can't ask Dirty Red lying in his grave—he couldn't read *illiterate* to save his too-young life.

Base began a revolution no one imagined, steeped in vials with red caps, plastic baggies, aluminum foil—and years later, imagine we abused ourselves seeking a stairway to utopia in a locale called Dodge City, better known as Washington, DC. Real? Damn straight. Follow the scent of destruction; blame it on base. It was the slow closing of a decade—family units losing the poor father, and the dear mother offering her body (the sinful flesh) on 13th and Logan Circle, prepared to violate herself with a trick or john. This is a place where tragic memories of the dead and affected pile up day after day—an unforgettable tale.

It is indeed difficult to adequately articulate the ambiance and temperament in DC created by the cocaine explosion of the '80s and its lasting impact on contemporary America.

Feature films and television series have attempted to re-create this problematic decade, the beginnings of what would later be referred to as the crack epidemic, through the eyes of a young Black man, showing hustlers hustling and grinding, the levels of addiction, and the resulting subculture. Often I have watched these programs with the aim of punching holes in the storylines presented, from terminology and mannerism to accuracy and credibility, through the eyes of a participant. I'm usually not impressed with these examinations of drug culture, though I wonder if an accurate depiction can be achieved at all.

The FX series *Snowfall*, created and directed by John Singleton, is perhaps the first to delve into the complicated layers of the crack epidemic without sensationalizing the storylines to the point of unbelievability. *Snowfall* provides the socioeconomic context that explains why so many Black men, women, trans, and queer-identified individuals fell victim to the fool's gold that infiltrated their neighborhoods and communities. Singleton uses as backstory the CIA's involvement with the Iran-Contra scandal, how operatives flooded Los Angeles with product to fund a war in another part of the globe and created the gateway for cocaine to make a lasting impact on Black communities throughout the United States. The narrative focuses on the protagonist Franklin and his relationship with a CIA operative who offers Franklin the chance to rise above his circumstances by selling large quantities of cocaine. Franklin quickly discovers how to heighten the power of the drug by turning the powder into ready rock. Lives are destroyed and family units broken, and the viewer witnesses it all through the eyes of Franklin.

Watching *Snowfall* reminds me of the wreckage I witnessed and lived through between 1980 and 1990 in DC. I witnessed too many lives destroyed and people killed.

The fact that I am a version of the main character does not escape me, but I never thought the white powder I smuggled into the United States was in some way connected to the military or the CIA, or that there was an intended outcome for someone other than myself. Was there an unseen puppet master pulling strings to direct my actions? There is only

one person I know who might be able to answer this question while
providing more background on how cocaine was smuggled from South
America to the States. JC resides in Hatchet Bay, Eleuthera, which was a
midway fueling and staging site for drug cartels during most of the '80s.
I often think about the devastation wrought in places like Memphis, Birmingham, and Washington, DC, and the role that I might have played
in the carnage, but I am also interested in learning what my friend knew
about the government's involvement in the drug trade, particularly on
the East Coast.

In 2019, this question, which had never occurred to me before, placed
me on a 6:00 A.M. JetBlue flight from Newark to Fort Lauderdale, then
to North Eleuthera via Silver Airways. I wanted to write about JC's
experience smuggling drugs here, a valuable but seldom-heard point of
view as the United States begins to explore the roots of the problem in
the '80s. Someday, the information from JC might be useful in a book
I hope to write retracing the steps cocaine travels from production to
transportation and delivery.

Upon arrival, I am met by Wilkie, the son of my late friend Ben, who
first introduced me to JC, and we drive to the township of Hatchet Bay.
I then check in with Minerva, Ben's widow and Wilkie's mother, who
rents cottages by the sea. Staying with Minerva is like staying with a
praying Black mother. She makes my meals and keeps telling me over
and over that she likes the new me, the changed man. "God is good,
Randall."

The breeze in the bay brushes my face slowly, methodically, as I
watch the water lap against the beach. The crystal-blue Bight of Eleuthera reaches for and makes contact with the shore's uneven edge—the
sand and the coral—only to be spit back into a collective mass of hydrogen and oxygen essential to breathe. The evening walk from Minerva's
cottage along the coral rock at the edge of the sand brings me back to
the same writing desk I had used in the past, a wooden picnic table offering a front-row seat to the ocean's horizon. Five years ago I sat in this
exact location, contemplating the relationship between space, time, and,
ultimately, the human existence while writing a letter to an incarcerated
friend at Metropolitan Detention Center in Brooklyn.

Today, as the sun begins to fade, I remember certain snippets of my
life in the '80s that eventually sent me to prison. I think about all the
lives I have fucked up, including my own. What fuels this memory is

the shipwrecked eyes of addicts and street hustlers who became the casualties of what we now know to be a deliberate attempt to cripple a particular group of people. Remorse for my role in this narrative seems to have drawn me back to the island, along with the hope that I might be resurrected like the ocean foam—dissolved into something brand new, perhaps a new way of being. *Why are you here?* the sea seems to ask me with each incoming wave. I have no answer. Maybe the stagnant clouds over the bay are a metaphor for my not knowing.

An aerial photograph from a twin-engine plane would reveal that my writing desk was located on the smooth surface of the hatchet in Hatchet Bay—the curved tip meant to dislodge and disfigure. Maybe I need to finally detach myself from the memory.

Privileged with the gift of surviving the white bloom, I can look back and take note of the carnage, the flashpoint that caused bodies to swell prisons to and beyond capacity.

After checking in with Minerva, I go to see JC to catch up a bit before meeting him again the next day on a dock in Hatchet Bay to hear his story.

JC and his brother, Morgan, were among the first wave of smugglers to follow Carlos Lehder, the original cocaine cowboy, who went to jail in 1984. JC and Morgan disproved the myths that Black people lacked access to airplanes or boats and that they were not allowed to participate in the intricate drug networks that flooded many US cities. While talking with me in Hatchet Bay five years earlier, JC told me how he became part of a national and international drug narrative, and it hinged on luck.

One day, JC was sitting outside on the front steps of his apartment in Nassau when a drunken-looking guy was attacked by two dogs who had been unleashed by their owner. After the attack, the owner whistled and the canines came running back to their master, leaving the drunken-looking guy on the pavement. He later got up, like a phoenix rising from the ashes, found a big brick, ran to the corner, and, instead of hitting the man with the dogs, threw the brick into a police car window. The police officers exited their vehicle, looking to lock the drunken-looking guy up. JC had witnessed the attack, so he hopped off the front porch and relayed the incident to the police, saving the man from jail.

The next day, the man meandered down the street while JC was again sitting outside on the steps; this time, however, Morgan was there too.

Morgan mentioned that the man was a crazy drunk who frequently talked about having access to cocaine in Colombia, though nobody believed him. JC caught up with the man, and they headed straight to the phone booth. Soon after, fifteen hundred pounds of cocaine arrived in Hatchet Bay. I met JC for the first time two years later, in 1986.

Now, JC and I are on the dock of Hatchet Bay, standing under the bow of a wrecked boat to shelter ourselves from the sun's midday heat. JC has concentrated solely on his fishing business since returning home from a four-year prison stint a while back; his fishing vessel is in the water, resting starboard on the pier's edge while both its engines are being overhauled. Two men are positioned deep within its hull, preparing the engines to be lifted out by crane. The crab season begins in two weeks, but JC and his crew are racing to get crab traps out early so that they will be ahead of the game. The crabs will be brought back to JC's processing plant just outside Hatchet Bay, to be packaged and shipped to various locations throughout the Bahamas.

When I first met JC more than thirty years ago, he was involved in the drug trade but equally committed to his work as a fisherman. The blond-red dreadlocks have since been replaced with a receding hairline, and age has thickened the midsection of his once-thin frame. Although I want to inquire about Morgan's sudden death a couple of years ago, it may still haunt JC, so it is a subject I do not bring up. We talk again about the days when we first met and the wild nature of drug smuggling before it matured with the advent of technology.

On my first visit to Eleuthera in 1986, JC entrusted me with a large package of drugs.

I had come to the island with fifteen hundred dollars, intending to purchase half a kilo. After laughing at my feeble gesture, JC fronted me a far larger package worth more than twenty thousand dollars. I would come to discover that the sum fronted was chump change for JC; it wouldn't even put a dent in his pocket. For me, however, it meant everything, and I vowed never to betray his trust.

On the dock at Hatchet Bay, we are about to have the kind of conversation that journalists in the United States and the Caribbean have sought from JC in the past. He has always refused to talk to them, but since we have a history together, he knows and trusts me. JC begins to tell his story, and it sounds hilarious, like the kind of fluke-type shit that no one would believe—but I do, because I know that JC is not a liar.

In 1989, an Aero Commander flew from North Eleuthera to La Guajira Peninsula in Colombia, the northernmost tip of South America, to pick up a cocaine shipment of more than three thousand pounds.

After the plane landed and was loaded with cargo, it took off and began heading to the city of Maicao. It developed engine trouble along the way, and the pilot had to land in the desert. A convoy arrived within the hour to assist JC and the other occupants of the plane so that they could reach Maicao along with their shipment.

Out of nowhere, a military helicopter appeared from the expansive sky, its blades hovering over the convoy, the carriage holding steady as it lowered to a resting place on the brownish sand. US military personnel disembarked, and JC noticed ribbons and medals adorning some of their uniforms.

The upper brass had a conversation with one of the occupants of the disabled plane, and soon afterward, half the cocaine was transferred to the helicopter. No one was arrested, and no money changed hands. After the last duffle bag was loaded, the military men reboarded the aircraft and closed its doors, and the helicopter took off as silently as it had arrived, bound for Quantico, Virginia.

When JC mentions military involvement, he speaks as if it's a known fact. Hearing this, I am sweating bullets on the pier under the boat because I had suspected government involvement and am now being proven right by an eyewitness. There were unseen puppet masters controlling the strings of the cocaine narrative in the '80s, and the ones who fell victim were totally unaware of the intended consequences.

After the helicopter disappeared, JC and the other occupants of the downed plane rode the convoy to Maicao, where they were provided with another aircraft. They took off from the city airport and headed north by northwest, eventually reaching Cuban territory, where they dropped the remaining duffle bags into the Caribbean Sea. Each kilo inside was wrapped in fiberglass to ensure that the product wouldn't get wet, and the fact that the shipment was dropped in Cuban waters almost guaranteed that it would be undetected by the US Coast Guard and US Drug Enforcement Administration.

At the spot where the cocaine was dropped, the crew of a seventeen-foot cigarette boat retrieved the bags, loaded them onto their vessel, and raced toward Miami. The following day the cocaine was transported to

West Palm Beach, where it was stuffed into a fleet of commercial trucks with hidden compartments.

As the vehicles traveled up the I-95 corridor through Georgia, South Carolina, North Carolina, Virginia, the District of Columbia, Maryland, and New Jersey into New York, the drivers avoided detection because their trucks blended into a society that prized commerce and capitalism, whereas lower-level dealers, the ones unable to afford planes and boats and trucks, were profiled, stopped, frisked, illegally searched, and sent to jail. Many did make it through the series of traps set by local police and state troopers, but they would have to pay four times the original price while assuming the risks and dangers of selling on the street.

Some of the trucks continued on to a small town in upstate New York just south of the Canadian border. On the other side of the border, another group of trucks stood by, identical in color, make, and model to the ones on the US side. Each morning a truck carrying concealed kilos crossed the border into Canada, as if going to do commercial work. In the evening, an identical truck crossed back into the United States with a legitimate commercial load, only it was not the same truck that crossed in the morning.

This is the story I hear from JC as we watch a crane lift an engine out of his boat. I am still stuck on "military."

The day before, I talked to a man coming to fix Minerva's cable service. I tell him that I am in Eleuthera to work on a book, and, without knowing the book's topic, he discloses that he has a screenplay by a now-deceased Eleuthera man who witnessed several instances of military involvement with cocaine shipments from the island of Norman's Cay to America. My friend Francis, who owns the Front Porch restaurant in North Eleuthera, reports a similar story. These unsolicited accounts confirm a Bahamian anticolonial consciousness similar to Langston Hughes's "so-called common element" of Blackness in America. The stories are often restated by everyday people, like the smooth-skinned gentleman who sells conch salad from a stand by the sea in Gregory Town.

What becomes evident in JC's story is that he does not harbor the same concern I do about being part of the problem. In the eyes of many on this island, JC gets a pass because his business ventures helped people thrive during a time when the Bahamas faced severe economic challenges often brought on by the United States' appetite for drugs. My point of view about drugs is an American one, colored by the divisiveness of capitalism; the American Black thinks differently from the Bahamian Black in many respects.

That evening, I sit at the bar at Francis's restaurant. The owner fixes me a plate of steamed crab, peas, and rice while I tell him about the project I am working on. Francis has heard the whispers about how the US government played a role in allowing drugs to devastate and disrupt America's urban centers and Black communities, a fact hard to verify in the court of public opinion. While I am eating, Francis is adamant about showing me an online video about the first prime minister of the Bahamas, Sir Lynden Oscar Pindling.

He is often referred to by Bahamians as the Father of the Nation, having led the successful campaign for independence from Great Britain in 1973. Toward the end of Pindling's tenure as prime minister, there were serious allegations that he allowed Carlos Lehder and the Medellín drug cartel to set up shop in Norman's Cay, where they proceeded to saturate the United States with cocaine. Lehder testified in his trial in 1987 that he made payments to Pindling and the Bahamian government, although Pindling had already been cleared of bribery charges after an investigation by the Royal Commission of Inquiry into Drug Trafficking and Government Corruption.

Pindling had appointed the Bahamian commission in response to the furor caused by an NBC News report entitled *The Bahamas: A Nation for Sale*, which aired in 1983. Narrated by investigative journalist Brian Ross, the broadcast alleged that Pindling and other government officials accepted bribes from drug smugglers including Lehder and had allowed the Bahamas to be used for the flow of drugs into the United States. In actuality, according to JC, Francis, and many others on the island, the United States itself helped to create, if not singlehandedly created, the problem. Given the information that has been revealed over the years about the FBI's counterintelligence program COINTELPRO and its subversion of the Black Panther Party and other radical Blacks in America, it would not be a stretch to believe that the United States' propaganda machine would go to great lengths to make Pindling the fall guy for something the federal government allowed to flourish.

In the clip Francis shows me, which is excerpted from the documentary *On the Wings of Men*, Pindling turns his back on Brian Ross while talking to Jane Pauley on his right. Pindling refuses to acknowledge Ross's presence, and the viewer can instantly sense the pure hatred he has for Ross. Pindling flat-out accuses Ross of journalistic misconduct when he states, "Mr. Ross is a faker. He has been known to conduct fraudulent interviews before. I don't want to deal with him." At the heart of the news segment used in *On the Wings of Men*, Pindling provides damning insight into the ongoing friction between the Bahamas and the United States:

> My little country stretches five, six hundred miles from Florida to Haiti or Cuba. In order for our tourism to grow, . . . we've got about twenty-five or twenty-six government-owned airstrips. . . . The FBI, the DEA, and any other kind of "A" you have, can't stop them coming into airfields in Florida. You expect my little country—me, with two hundred-odd thousand people—to be able to do what you can't do in this big country [the United States]? Y'all gotta be crazy!

The word on the street in the Bahamas, as told to me by Francis, is that if Pindling had won his reelection bid in 1992, there was a Navy SEAL team waiting to carry out an assassination attempt on his life. Fact or fiction, we may never know. But Francis is adamant about this possible outcome. Though some would call Francis's statement conjecture, I know all too well about the stories hidden underneath the dominant narrative of whiteness in Black America. One thing for certain, and two for sure: JC's experience is not conjecture, and I believe the story he told me about the US military's involvement in the Colombian transaction.

The next day I am scheduled to catch a Silver Airways flight leaving North Eleuthera at 3:45 P.M., with a stop in Fort Lauderdale before arriving in Newark at 9:00 P.M.

Wilkie drives me back down Queen's Highway to the airport. It is difficult to say good-bye to a paradise I see through American eyes. As soon as we pass Gregory Town, we have to cross the Glass Window Bridge to continue north (the bridge spans the meeting point of the Atlantic and the Bight of Eleuthera), and, for the first time in all of my visits, I understand the duality of this picturesque scene. Although I've crossed this bridge many times during my travels, this time I am able to feel and sense the metaphor within the image that the Glass Window represents. I am now able to inhale and exhale the past. Forgive and let go, confront and reconcile. Perhaps it is the only way to abnegate two colliding images pushing forth a generation in which I lost myself, never understanding the unseen puppet master on the scene, manipulating the strings to a choice I made. I now contemplate whether I even had a choice at all.

Here exists a new way of looking—on either side of the bridge: hydrogen and oxygen, elements to a gateway—a window into the dichotomy of how we live or sound, or both. The rugged and the harsh mirrored by the calm and the serene, converging only to run away from each other. The rattling glass vial of powder mixed with baking soda in a boiling pot to produce a beige rock.

Three for twenty-five, sixteenths, eight-balls, and sixty-twos, a commodity dictated by grams—the alleys and storefront crevices harboring those looking for a come-up—sixteen bullets to the dome and my friend's body in a bathtub on 16th Street in Northwest DC. An accidental or intended point of view: the two bodies of water, an arrival and a departure, a reconfigured memory out of a past event—the damage done. The problem is mine alone to let go.